Poor

Poor

*Grit, courage, and the life-changing
value of self-belief*

Katriona O'Sullivan

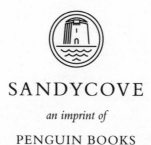

SANDYCOVE

an imprint of

PENGUIN BOOKS

SANDYCOVE

UK | USA | Canada | Ireland | Australia
India | New Zealand | South Africa

Sandycove is part of the Penguin Random House group of companies
whose addresses can be found at global.penguinrandomhouse.com.

First published 2023

004

Copyright © Katriona O'Sullivan, 2023

The moral right of the author has been asserted

Set in 13.5/17.75pt Perpetua Std
Typeset by Jouve (UK), Milton Keynes
Printed and bound in Great Britain by Clays Ltd, Elcograf S.p.A.

The authorized representative in the EEA is Penguin Random House Ireland,
Morrison Chambers, 32 Nassau Street, Dublin D02 YH68

A CIP catalogue record for this book is available from the British Library

ISBN: 978–1–844–88621–0

To me, aged seven.
I've got you.

Author's Note

To protect people's privacy a number of names in this book have been changed, including those of my siblings. I have also changed some identifying details. At the back of the book there is a list of all names that are pseudonyms.

Prologue

I heard what the doctor said and so did my dad. But by the time we went down the two flights of stairs and out into the portico, my father had reshuffled the cards.

'If you give up smoking now, Tony,' the oncologist had said, 'you've a good chance of beating this.'

Dad pulled out a cigarette as soon as our feet got over the entrance. He lit up, pushed the lighter back among the cigarettes in the box of Bensons and put it back into the pocket of his shirt. He always wore short-sleeved check shirts, my dad.

I stared at him in disbelief. He noticed and lifted his chin, put his shoulders back, dragged on his cigarette and blew the smoke out through his nose.

'Dad . . .'

He switched his grip, changed the cigarette from between two fingers to his finger and thumb. He broadened his shoulders again, straightened up. He was not a tall man so this was how he got height between you when he was defensive.

'The doctor said you've to give up smoking, Dad,' I said.

But he shook his head, pressed his mouth into a line. He looked away.

'No, that's not what he said.' My father was well spoken. 'I've to cut back a bit, that's all.'

Jesus Christ.

Tony O'Sullivan, my dad, was gone in less than a year.

But I lost him right there. Standing right there outside the hospital in his cloud of smoke and denial, for me, it was all over. I could say I snapped, but that's not the truth. I unfurled, in the way those huge cables that hold up bridges do during an earthquake. The thousands of wires, all the little connections I had made to this man, they quietly snapped one by one.

All the people I had ever been, the three-year-old, the seven-year-old, the fifteen-year-old me. We all stood there staring, finally realizing, finally getting it.

He doesn't care.

We *are* unloved, he doesn't care.

Nothing mattered to Tony O'Sullivan. I didn't, standing in front of the hospital heartbroken at the news that my father was so ill, realizing that his plan was to smoke himself to death. Nobody mattered to him and never had. Not us kids, not my mother, not our childhood or the struggle, none of it. At that moment, nothing mattered to Tony except that smoke in his hand. He knew it; I knew it. Everything we had ever been through meant – *fuck's sake* – nothing to him. None of it, none of us.

My dad was an addict.

And as all those dreamed-up attachments I had made through wishful thinking twisted and fell away, I was left standing on the far side, the furthest I had ever been from this impossible man, this waste of brains and spirit. This man I had spent my whole life desperately loving. He lived for his addictions. Those cigarettes, like his heroin, booze and women – my dad's addictions *were* him.

He flicked his cigarette ash and it landed on the ground between us. I looked at it. There was not going to be a eureka moment, not for Tony. He would free-fall into this fire until the end. There was nothing I could do about it. He was not going to rise from the ashes.

All of this, all of it, had been for nothing. I was the only phoenix, the only one of the two of us who would make it out of this mess. The changes, the lessons, the climb out of the stinking trench I was born into, that was just for me. Just me.

Just me.

And that is the saddest thing I ever knew.

I

There are memories I want to keep. Memories I am happy to talk about. Sitting in the rear seat of my dad's green Cortina in the summer, looking at the back of his head, his mop of curls, window down, his brown arm resting on the door with a cigarette between his fingers. The way the rushing air hits my face like a fan, and my hair whips against my cheeks. My dad's tapes are playing, my whole family are singing. My dad's gold ring tapping against the metal.

And there are memories I want to let go of, ones I find it hard to talk about. Memories that weigh me down. I want to tell you about those too, so I can leave them here and move on from them.

Standing, aged six, at the door to my parents' bedroom looking in. My eyes hadn't adjusted to the light, not quite, so I couldn't figure out what I was looking at.

Then I could.

My dad was on his bed at an angle. His jeans were half off, and I could see his tummy and his underwear. There were black rings all over his skin and one purple bruise spreading across his thigh with a plastic syringe – the type he put in his arm – stuck in the middle of it. The tube part of it lolled downwards, pinned by the needle.

I stood looking. The bed he lay on was stained yellow with piss and one beam of sunlight crossed the floor through the old curtains that were pulled shut and across his body, lighting him up. Dust floated in the light.

His face was turned to me.

Dead?

Did I say it out loud? *Dead?* I think I called it out, but I didn't know. The sound looped around, and I couldn't place my own voice over the loud beat of my heart.

I must have been calling out, looking back, because my dad's friend John Bean clattered through the house, taking the stairs three at a time to the top, pulling on a jumper as he careered down the landing. He pushed me behind him and crossed the bedroom, saying my dad's name over and over.

'Hey, Tony, hey hey, Tony . . .'

'Is Dad dead?' I said.

John Bean rushed past me, down the stairs and into the street.

My dad, Tony O'Sullivan, was born in Ireland. The first five years of his life are unknown. We just know he was handed in to the infamous Goldenbridge industrial school by his mother and stayed there until he was five. He was adopted by Jim and May O'Sullivan and taken to live in their home in Clontarf. They had no other children. My grandfather Jim was a civil servant, though he had studied medicine in UCD. He had a strong faith, went to Mass every day and always read the *Irish Times* from cover to cover.

My dad told us that when Jim was dying he asked him for information about his origins. Jim told him that his aunt, Sister Francis Xavier (Jim's sister), was his mother. Tony had known this aunt through his childhood, through family get-togethers that would happen once a year. She had been generous with gifts for him on those days, and yet he said their interactions would always leave him feeling upset and stressed.

The story he was told, at the end of it all, was that she became pregnant at forty-two, in the convent where she lived in Cork, and so the baby was brought to the Goldenbridge in Dublin by another of Jim's sisters, also a nun. Tony was adopted, at what age or for how long we don't know, and then returned there. When he was five his uncle, Jim, took him home.

My dad took that story very badly.

But Tony made it all up. As I was completing work on this book I took a DNA test. It revealed that I have no genetic connection with the O'Sullivans. God knows why he came up with that yarn but by the time Jim died stories about the abuse of children in Goldenbridge had come out. Maybe Tony could not take the idea that he was one of those kids and, with his father no longer around to contradict him, he made up this fairy tale of being protected by the nuns.

We don't know what happened to Tony in the first five years of his life, but as more stories come out about Catholic-run charity organizations in the fifties and sixties, it's not hard to imagine.

But we do know that in that time, before he got his lovely middle-class family, his civil-servant father and his stay-at-home mother, Tony lost something.

And he never got it back.

Tony used to tell us kids that his first memories were of a fire. He told us he was standing up in a cot crying as fire raged all around him.

'I don't know where I came from,' he would say, 'but I know I was in a fire.'

I used to run that image through my head a lot as a kid, that baby in a fire. Standing on his feet in a cot, watching everything fall apart and burn to the ground, and not able to help himself.

Whether it was the truth or something else my dad made up, well, we will never know. He probably made it up; he made up a lot of stuff.

As a teenager Tony was a free spirit who rebelled against the middle-class life his parents wanted for him. They gave him everything he needed to make it, but he didn't want it. They lived in a peaceful home on the coast. He attended a private boys' school in the middle of Dublin, Belvedere College, where he was a tennis champion. He was offered a place in Trinity College, but he rejected it and went to England instead to sell paintings door to door and do drugs.

My dad told me that when he was a boy he would cycle from his house to Dollymount Strand, and he would lie in the grass, smoking and reading his books. He said that was his favourite thing to do. I think he told me that story because that was the real him, the real Tony, there on the beach with his head resting on an upturned saddle. I like to think of him there, in Dublin Bay, with gulls surfing above him calling to one another. I can see him in my mind's eye, shielding his eyes from the sun with his book. That was Tony before he got caught up in a spiral of addiction, running from whatever it was he lost in those first five years. Maybe the quiet on that beach got too quiet, maybe he had to get out of his head because of what haunted him in there. Who knows? Before long he met my mother at a bus stop in Coventry and not long after that they had five children and addictions they couldn't handle and a life of the grimmest misery you could ever imagine. When he arrived in England, Tony had only ever dabbled in drugs. But by the time I was six years old and standing in the doorway looking across at his lifeless body, half on and half off the bed, he was a heroin addict.

Tony was middle class and an educated man. He was well spoken, charismatic and carried himself well.

He was also a career criminal, an alcoholic and a junkie.

And he was *my* dad.

John Bean had gone for help. My dad had overdosed and was dying, lying on a bed covered in piss and vomit. This was the way of our house. The ambulance men came in and they didn't hurry. They were bored of this, it seemed. They took the steps with the urgency of men heading to bed, one step at a time, huffing and puffing. They looked at my dad in the room and shifted around, looking at each other with sideways glances and raised eyebrows.

I knew that code, the language of the scornful. I knew how to read that language already, at six years of age. My dad was lying there dying and, even though it was their job to care, they didn't think he was worth saving.

They were rough with him. 'Up you get, fella,' one of them said as if he had just taken a tumble. They pulled him by his legs and arms and swung him on to the stretcher sideways, awkwardly, so he lay on it with one arm under his ribs. One of them shoved his leg up and his shoe fell off. That man rolled his eyes and kicked the shoe under the bed. He mumbled something and the other man rolled his eyes too.

They didn't want to help. They didn't want to help my dad.

I shook my head back and forth at the scene in front of me and I was crying, but I didn't say anything. I wanted to shout at them to save my dad, help him. But I didn't. I just wiped the tears off my chin with my sleeve. It was soaking wet.

John paced around. 'Is he all right?' he said to one of the paramedics and was ignored. It was as if he wasn't there.

'Is my dad dead?' I asked the other man. He ignored me.

The stretcher with my dad on it was brought past me and down the stairs. It felt like I was watching it all play out, but it wasn't real. I thought over and over, *Dead?*

He looked dead. His skin was grey and taut, and his eyes were sunk back into the bones of his skull. He was so pale I could see the red hairs of his moustache as if individually, and the details of his skin, the blue fading veins in his hands, his little finger with his sovereign ring.

'Dad . . .' I said.

They got him out of the house. And then he was gone, the ambulance was gone. They didn't flash the lights or put the siren on.

I thought about the marks on my dad's legs, the blue and purple blotches on his white skin. The black and grey rings. I knew they were from the needles.

John Bean went down the stairs. I followed.

'Don't worry, K,' he said, and I nodded.

'Is Dad dead?' I said.

'No, no, just a bit rough,' John said. He pushed his trainers off with a toe into each heel and sat down. 'Your dad will be all right, don't be worrying. Tilly will be back soon as well so . . .'

He patted the couch beside him. But I didn't sit. I went back up the stairs and looked at the bed where my dad had been.

If Dad was dead, who would drive us in the car?

Tony didn't die. He came back later that day and pretended to everyone that he was fine, though you could see the wear and tear behind his eyes. When he sat down on the couch I ran and got him a lighter and his cigarettes from where they had fallen on the floor upstairs.

'Ah thanks, my Katriona,' he said.

He always said that to me.

We were glad to see him. He shook John Bean's hand and they gassed back and forth between the two of them.

'Thought you were finished, Tone,' John said.

'Not me, John,' Dad said, smiling through the smoke he was exhaling. He pulled extra hard on the cigarette for the next drag.

The day after, the sun was shining and my dad let me sit in the car and pretend to drive it. He rolled down the windows and shut me in and stood back, smoking, while I strained my neck to look in the rear-view mirror, sliding my hands round the leather wheel. I pulled the gear stick back and forth and bounced on the seat. Sunlight filled the car and I felt as though I was being fed by it. My dad closed his eyes and tilted his face towards the light, and I watched him breathe in and out. Then he looked at me and his face creased into a smile.

'Want some music?' He leaned in and put the key into the ignition and turned the tape player on. The tape was Fleetwood Mac, the song was 'Go Your Own Way'. This was our song.

When he was like that I loved my dad more than anyone in the whole world.

2

Some of my earliest memories are of my little neighbour Katie and me chasing after our older siblings, desperately trying to keep up with them as they desperately tried to lose us. It was a regular event.

Only this one time I got hit by a car.

We lived on Vine Street, a long narrow street, lined on one side with houses and on the other side with huge pitches belonging to the Sidney Stringer School. The school itself was at the very end of the road, across from the church. Behind our house there used to be a wasteland, backing on to a graveyard belonging to St Peter's, but I hear they're both gone – there are houses there now.

The area is Hillfields, described by the press as the frontline of Coventry. It's one of the poorest places in Great Britain. Back then, despair was around us in every direction, as though the poor had been corralled here, to keep us all together and out of sight.

In our area everyone was from somewhere else, and

that's how we organized ourselves. Caribbean, Nigerian, Asian, Scottish and Irish. We all mingled and loved each other just as much as we fought, but – as is the way of immigrants – we felt more attached to our own. My dad always sought out other Irish no matter where we were. Being Irish in Britain is never easy, certainly not in the seventies and eighties during the IRA campaigns. The Irish felt the backlash of that for years. My dad did anyway; he was pulled in over the 1974 Birmingham bombings.

The horizon of Hillfields was broken in places by high-rise flats, like tombstones against the skyline. They were the worst sort of high-rise, the kind with stains around the edges. My mum's friend Helen jumped off those flats.

Everyone around us was in the thick of it. We had nothing. So as it tends to in places like that, alcohol and drugs took hold of most people. It's what kept them going. Mad as that seems to say, that's how it was. Drugs and alcohol kept people going until it outran them, and that's how it was for us too, over and over. In our house, most of the time, every spoon was singed black from cooking gear.

Smoking weed – we called it draw – was as normal as having a cup of tea in Hillfields. But anything to do with gear was covered up. I learned early on to stay out of the kitchen when my parents were both in there with the door shut. At first, they smoked it, sending me to the shop for Milkybars, those little white chocolate bars wrapped in silver foil and paper. I just thought they liked the chocolate, but they were after the foil. Then, later, they injected. I sometimes found them passed out, so stoned that all they could do was slump, a needle in their arm or leg. That was the way it was from the time I was really small.

Banging up was something to be ashamed of and I somehow picked up on that social rule, even though my own parents had always done it. It was in the way they shouted 'Get out!' if you walked in on them. It was in the way they hid the bag under the corner of the carpet. It was wrong – I knew it and so did they. But even so, I saw heroin, for a long time, as a medicine that kept my mum well. It was the only solution to her vomiting and shitting; it put an end to her twisting and screeching.

We knew everyone who lived on our road. The Dixons, where the dad killed their dog in a temper one night with a machete. The Patels, with the disabled kid. The Clarkes, where each boy had a different dad. The Clarkes' mum was my mum's friend Bett, who used to come over to our house and get so drunk she would wet herself on our couch. She always denied it but one time my mother discovered the wet patch straight away, just after Bett had left, and was so enraged she marched down to Bett's house with a can of green paint and wrote the words 'FAT SLAG' on her front door.

The police called in to our house around twenty minutes later. 'What did you think you were doing down the road, Tilly?' they asked my mum, and she said she didn't know what on earth they were referring to. They showed her the green footprints leading from Bett's house, straight to our door.

At the back of our terraced houses we all shared a green space. It was through the gate of our little fenced-off yards, a wide stretch of grass that ran down to a copse of huge oak trees. They must have been hundreds of years old. When I deliberately focus on positive images from my childhood I think of those trees, the way the sunshine on the grass ended abruptly in their dark shade, the way your eyes would adjust as you ran under them. I see myself running down the green, the shape of my brother's legs swinging down from the branches. Next door to us was a red-haired family called Gallagher, who were Irish too. The Gallagher and O'Sullivan houses were cemented together in more ways than one: they had kids the same ages as us and the youngest, Katie, was my best friend. Her sisters, Amy and Sharon, were the same ages as my brothers. My memories of her are the two of us on our hunkers out the back, making pies in the mud, or daisy chains, and of course chasing the older ones. We were so little.

Every day, throughout the day, like little pins in my already deflating soul, Mrs Gallagher would call out for Katie.

'Katie love, come for lunch.'

'Katie love, come eat your dinner.'

'Katie love, it's getting cold, come get a jumper on.'

And Katie would jump up and run along the path to her house, to her mum standing in the doorway. She would run into her mum's legs and hold them, and her mother would bend over and give her head a cuddle and a kiss.

And I would feel it.

With every cuddle Katie got, it was like I lost another one. The way her mum was showed me what my mum was not. Katie had a real mum and I didn't. Mine was broken.

When Katie was coming out to play, dressed well in her little check skirts and white socks, her mum would watch her run down the yard to me and wait until she met me, and that door stayed ajar.

My mum was never at our door. Our door was shut.

Both mums often instructed the older kids to take us with them.

My mum would tell Michael, 'Look after your sister,' but he never wanted to, and Katie's older sisters were the same. They wanted to go off to where the big kids hung out and we were getting in their way. So they always ran off, but we would run after them for as far as we could until we lost them. Then we would stop and play wherever they lost us, until they came back. I never told on them. It was a rule to never tell on my brothers.

That was the story when I got hit by the car.

It wasn't far from our house, just down the way. I was chasing my brothers, Katie in tow, when they disappeared through the fence at the school.

'James! Michael! Mum said play with –' I shouted after them, cut short by a heavy force that threw me off my feet into the air and landed me on my front with a smack on the tarmac, about five feet from the bumper of a yellow Fiat Uno.

I rolled on to my back, winded. A candyfloss cloud chugged across the blue sky and a man's face interrupted the view of it. I groaned.

'Hey, sweetheart, hey, pet,' he said in a half-whisper. I noticed beads of sweat on his cheeks. He crouched down and felt along the back of my neck, across my shoulders and down my arms.

'Can you see me?' He waved his hand. 'Can you move? Wiggle your toes.' He pressed the toes through my shoes. I couldn't wiggle my toes at all because my shoes were far too small, so I wiggled my legs instead. The man put his arms under me and lifted me up, over to the path, and laid me down again. He moved with care.

My little friend Katie, aged four like me, crouched down beside me and said in a quiet and motherly voice, 'Oh, Katriona, you did get hit off the car.' She pronounced my name, as most around me did, *Cat-tree-oh-nah*.

I heard my mum before I saw her.

She was shouting 'No! No! No!' as she ran down from our house. As she reached me she clearly saw I was still alive so she flew past me to where my brothers were standing, wide-eyed and white-faced, at the broken wall of the pitch, like yin and yang in their matching tracksuits of opposing colours. She crossed the road, fizzing with curses at them, before she turned round and flew back to me, down on her knees by my side, looking me over.

'Is she okay?' she asked the man. 'Are you okay?' she asked me. She looked from me to the man and back, then over her shoulder again. 'You little fuckers!' she roared at Michael and James, then she noticed Katie, 'Are you okay?', and back to me, 'Does anything hurt?' I nodded. My knees were burning and my forehead was stinging.

'I'm a doctor,' the man said, and my mum grabbed the sleeve of his jacket.

'Is she okay? Can you see if something's broken?' She ran her hand along each of my arms.

'She seems fine, she's all right,' the doctor said. His cheeks were bright pink. He lifted my arms and moved them, then pulled me gently up into a sit.

I took big breaths in and out. My mum scooped me up then and sat down with me on the kerb. I held on. She looked me over, like a mother with a new baby, checking my fingers, blowing on my scrapes, searching for injuries she had missed. Her hands were papery and warm. I said 'Ouch' so I could feel her hands again.

The doctor got me to stand up and wiggle my fingers and toes, and I told him how many fingers he was holding up. Three. I was proud when I got it right. Then he asked me to watch his finger and he moved it back and forth.

Katie told on my brothers. 'They didn't wait for Katriona,' she said, pointing at them like they were criminals in a line-up. 'Him and him didn't.' They stood there with open mouths.

'I can't believe you let this happen!' my mum shouted across at them. Then she said sorry to the man. She whooshed me up on to her hip as she swung round to shout at my brothers one more time, telling them they were in for it.

She carried me back to the house with my head on her shoulder and my legs round her waist. My fingertips pressed into her freckled shoulders and ran up into the strands of her hair that fell against her neck. I closed my eyes and smelled her skin.

She had an instinct, my mum, a sense of maternal love. It *was* in there. Problem was, you had to go under a car to feel it.

3

I don't remember my own first day of school at all. I just remember my brother Matthew's. I suppose the memories have merged, or mine are overshadowed and stored behind the day he had.

Matthew and I were the third and fourth children, born barely a year apart and like two peas in a pod for the first few years of our life. Everyone around called us 'Irish twins' and I thought that we genuinely were, not getting the joke until years later. We did everything together. What I liked, he liked; what he liked, I did. Of all the most fun times in my early childhood, Matthew is right there with me, his face so full of mischief and spirit right from the start. In the mornings we were always the first up and, long before we were really old enough to get ourselves to school, we would make ourselves sugar sandwiches, literally just bread and sugar, and head out to get there before any other kids so we would have the playground to ourselves. That independence was the key to solving the troubles that my brother Matthew brought to my second year in school;

as long as my mum brought him, he fought the system. Tooth and nail.

Nursery and Reception are the first two classes for children starting school in the UK. I was a year ahead of Matthew but in our school, Southfields Primary, the classes were all together in one large open-plan room, which meant we would share the same teacher.

By the time we got up the school steps on his first day, Matthew had started screaming, and as much as my mum pushed him on to his little chair at the circular desk where he was to sit, he pushed back. He hung on to her arm.

'Stop it, Matthew,' my mum said and looked over at me. What was I supposed to do? Why was I always dragged into this? All I wanted was to be here at school in my classroom with my lovely teacher. I wished that my mum would just go and take Matthew with her. School was my place.

One of the teacher's assistants, Miss Hall, walked over and took my brother by his two arms, pulling his hands off my mum and signalling to her to leave. My mum ran out of there.

Matthew lost his mind. He kicked the table and the chair, and the assistant teachers ran in circles after him as he slid and burrowed between other pupils in a bid to escape. Other children started crying too.

Then my teacher, Mrs Arkinson, came through the door with her brown leather book bag in one hand and her coat in the other. She stood for a moment taking in the screaming, hissing mess that was my brother. She raised a finger and with a firm 'Ah-ah!' she stopped him in his tracks. He looked at her, and she shook her head. 'There will be NO running in my classroom,' she said. 'Sit down.'

And he did. Although he still cried the whole day, face down into his arm at his desk. And every other day that year. He hated being away from my mum.

I didn't understand that at all and, frankly, I was raging. I was so happy to be going back to school after the summer. I liked the way things were set out there, always the same. And we got fed, with school dinners. If it wasn't for school I wouldn't have had a dinner, if I'm honest. Sometimes I would be given breakfast by Mrs Arkinson, if I was in the class early enough, before the others came in. Mrs Arkinson had a blue-and-orange metal cupboard and sometimes she would bring out a lunchbox from in there and pass me a bun or a fairy cake to get me through to lunch. But most days, by the time I heard the shutters of the canteen going up, the rumble echoing through the halls, my stomach would be growling and I'd lose concentration for whatever I was doing and instead focus on the delicious smells that wafted down from where the dinner ladies were setting up. There were five of them, dressed in white coats and hats, and they'd call out to you as you queued up, letting you know what was in. The queue never moved fast enough for me. There was a routine to school dinners, the same meal on the same day, and the food was made in big trays. Shepherd's pie, chicken pie, and mince and onions – that was my favourite – served with mashed potato and gravy poured on top from a big ladle. We would get roly-poly pudding on Thursdays. Other kids, the loved ones, they sometimes complained, but I didn't give a shit what was served, I'd have eaten anything. My mouth would water in advance as I moved up the queue, watching the dinner ladies slap portion after portion on to tray after tray until they got to me. The clank of knives and forks, the little cartons of milk, the good food: this was routine, every day the same. I would hear the call of 'Custahhd! Custahhd!' from the dinner lady at the end, a huge Cypriot woman with a strong accent, and feel at home. I would sit down at the plastic picnic-style tables, always the same one – across from two boys, both called Adam – and eat my food contentedly. The routines of school – the desk where I knew to sit, the timetable, my school dinners – that was what I needed.

I liked school. There was a place for me there. My name was on a list – Mrs Arkinson always checked if I was there and would tick my name.

'An Irish girl in my class, what a treat,' she said when I first started. 'I'm Irish too,' she added. I pulled my bottom lip between my teeth and chewed on it. I knew that *Irish* was something, it was what my dad was, and what my mum's dad was, though I wasn't quite sure what it meant. But if I had that in common with Mrs Arkinson, it must be treasure for sure.

'O'Sullivan means one-eyed, did you know that?' she said, pushing her chair back and pressing a badge with my name written across it in blue marker on to my chest. She patted it to make it stick.

I nodded. But I didn't know. I used to nod at everything she said.

'Two brothers back many years ago in ancient Ireland had a terrible fight,' she said, 'and one tore the other's eye out with a stick.' Her accent was stronger than my dad's. And warmer.

I thought about the fights that went on in our area, always as the sun dimmed and the drink of the day soured in hungry bellies. I could well believe the story about the brothers.

'Now,' she said, 'I'm glad you're in my class, one of my own.'

And she kept that going, all through my first year of school. I felt as though I was a favourite. I'm sure she made connections with all of the children; she had a knack. But it seemed there would always be an errand which I would do in earnest, a blackboard to wipe clean, or papers to hand out to the desks, or an important message written on a memo pad, folded and handed to me with instructions on how to get to where I had to hand it in.

I think we all have those teachers, the ones who like

us. As a child I had a strong, warm temperament – I can see the spark in my eyes when I look at photos of back then. I was driven and some teachers loved me for it. And, of course, some didn't.

I loved Mrs Arkinson and I knew she loved me. Her eyes said so. The way she helped me said so. The pat on my head, the hand on my shoulder, the encouragement and rewards. When Mrs Arkinson was pleased with you, well, you felt like you could survive forever on that small nod or pat on the head. It was like she pushed confidence into you.

One day in Reception she called me up and told me that Miss Hall was going to need to speak to me in the bathroom and that I was to listen to what she had to say and everything would be fine.

I'd seen looks between them already, just before I was called up, and I had my guard raised. I could always sense these things, the shift in the room when there was trouble brewing. My mind had instantly raced with excuses for things I'd done and for things I hadn't done. I prepared for all eventualities, knew who I would pass the blame to, what I would deny. Whatever I was accused of I would reject or ignore, and it would go away eventually. When Miss Hall came to get me, one of the other kids in my class said, 'You're for it now, Katriona O'Sullivan, whatever you done.'

When we got into the girls' loos Miss Hall pushed open all the cubicle doors and then pushed the handle back on the main door, locking us in. It was very unusual so I figured I must be in terrible trouble. I stared at the floor and flexed my feet against the lino.

She rummaged in the bag she had brought with her. She took out a pile of white things and laid them out on the tiles. Small, folded girls' pants, the way they are when you take them out of their plastic packet. She lined them up in a row.

Then I knew exactly what this was all about. Of course I did.

Pissy pants.

I was wetting the bed every single night – children tend to do that when they are in crisis – and then going to school without washing or changing my pants. I didn't know how to wash. There were no towels in our bathroom, barely any toilet paper. Never any soap. None of us owned a toothbrush.

In the toilets with Miss Hall I felt ashamed, as though it wasn't just the kids who teased and mocked me.

'*Pissy pants, pissy pants.*'

'*Smelly bitch.*'

'*I don't want to sit with Katriona, Miss, she smells like wee.*'

I knew that Mrs Arkinson and Miss Hall thought I was smelly too.

It was true. I stared at the floor. Couldn't she just leave me alone? I didn't want to talk about it. I didn't want to talk to anyone.

Miss Hall crouched down and said, quietly and kindly, 'Katriona, you're not in trouble, we are going to help.'

I did need help. I could sense it in the relief I felt from her words and looking at the pants. They had pictures of little girls in tea dresses on the front, and days of the week stamped above the picture.

'Monday, Tuesday, Wednesday, Thursday, Friday,' she said, landing her finger on each one as she said the word.

I looked at Miss Hall and she was looking at me. I wanted to reach out and touch her fluffy hair and silky blouse with the big loose bow at the neck of it. She was so clean and pretty and smelled lovely. I sometimes wondered if she could actually be Princess Diana, they looked the same to me. Maybe it was really her, a princess in our class.

'When you come into school in the morning, before everyone else, I want you to come to my desk and I will give you a set like this.' She showed me a white flannel and a white towel and lifted one pair of pants on to the small pile. 'You take them and come into the loo and lock the door like I just did, okay?'

I didn't nod or shake my head. I just stared at the floor.

'Do you wet the bed?' she asked, hunching to look up at my face. I flinched but didn't answer. She pushed my hair back.

'Head up now,' she said, 'nothing to be ashamed of, but let's learn to keep ourselves . . . fresh and clean.'

There were three little sinks and she chose the last one, explained how to run the water warm and then showed me how to wash.

'Start on our legs,' she said after I took off my yellow stained pants. She threw them into the bin straight away. 'Get the flannel wet in the warm water, then we twist like this so it won't drip, and now we rub our legs like this.' She showed me how, up and down from my knees.

The way she kept saying 'we' felt nice. I was never part of a 'we'.

'Head up, Katriona,' she reminded me. 'Nothing to worry about, we are learning how girls wash.' She wiped across my groin and around my hips and bum.

She showed me again, 'Up and down, wash wash wash, around and under,' and asked me to show her how to do it myself.

I did, repeating the words as she said them.

'Then dry like this,' she said, patting my skin and giving me the towel to repeat the action myself.

'Now pop on your Monday pants,' she said, handing them to me.

She repeated my new routine: I was to come in every day and use the girls' loo to wash like she'd showed me and put on my new pants. She would keep the pants in school and every morning she would give me the bundle of flannel and towel, and a pair of pants. My used pants went back into the little bag; there was a small stand in front of the cubicles and she showed me where to leave the bag when I was finished. I never thought about what happened to it after I left with my clean pants on, but of course it was making its way to Mrs Arkinson's washing machine and back into school for the following week.

I stood there in clean pants, with clean legs.

'Now,' she said, 'what a great girl.'

I felt as though I was standing in a beam of sunlight.

She will never know what she did for me, how in that small bundle of towel, flannel and pants, Miss Hall gave me power. In that small bathroom every morning, before the other girls came in, I was in control of one thing.

A few months after that Mrs Arkinson called me to the cloakroom during break time.

'Well, Katriona, guess what?' she said to me. She said my name the same way my dad did. *Cat-tree-nah*.

I answered with a shake of my head, then a nod; I didn't understand the question but I wanted to please her.

'I was walking in town yesterday –' she rummaged in a cubby, pulling out a folded plastic bag – 'and I passed a window and saw this.' She took out a roll of blue velvet and shook it out. It was a dress.

There was a white collar attached to the neckline, long sleeves and a pale blue thread in a zigzag along the hem.

'Isn't that lovely?' she said. 'Would you look at that dress now?'

'Is it for me?' I said, reaching out and touching the hem. It was soft. I held on.

'It is!' she said with a cheer. 'Isn't that just a perfect dress for you? I knew it when I saw it in the shop window.'

I nodded with as much enthusiasm as I could find, straightening my spine and smiling as wide as I could to make sure she could see it.

'So now, take that with you,' she said, putting it back into the bag and handing it to me. Then we walked back to the class, her ahead, me behind holding my bag tightly as if it would be whipped off me any minute. The other girls looked at me as I did. I stuck my tongue out. They didn't know what I'd got.

I wore that dress every day until it chafed my armpits and wouldn't close, and even then I still wore it. Putting it on and going into school felt like wearing armour. My teacher was my friend, I belonged here. Naturally, when Matthew arrived at my school – screaming and crying and making a fuss – I was so annoyed. He was ruining the one good thing I had. I stared over at him, wishing he would disappear. I bet Mrs Arkinson would realize that I was from no good and not like me any more.

'Now, Katriona,' Mrs Arkinson called out and I whipped my head round, 'would you run me an errand, please? I need a good, responsible girl to carry it out.'

I was so relieved.

*

Although it didn't register at the time, and wouldn't for years, from that small act of self-care Mrs Arkinson and Miss Hall taught me, somewhere deep down I understood that I could control my fate. Feeling clean and fresh was something that could be mine. As long as I had access to the tools I needed – the flannel and towel and help of my teacher – I could be in charge of that one thing. Every morning I stood in the little loo washing myself and replacing my stained pants with the new ones, and in many ways that was the start of finding my strength.

The little change of pants every day, the smile and pat on the head as I collected my bundle and made my way to the loo to wash, they were the beginnings of betterment. The new dress was a sign to me that people were good and kind, and that I was worthy of being cared for. I didn't understand that outright but somewhere it went in.

In Mrs Arkinson's class I felt like I had my feet on the ground and a backbone. I had a voice and choices to make. I had a brain. There were books there and I loved books. When I think back to what I was then, the small, undernourished child of two junkies, I know that I was lucky to have a very special teacher for my first few years in school. I deserved better than what I had because I *was* better than that. Mrs Arkinson could see it, Miss Hall too, and eventually I saw it myself.

I wasn't so lucky with teachers after that. Not in that school anyway.

4

There was a large brown bloodstain on our bathroom carpet that stayed there until we moved out, when I'd imagine the council ripped it up. It was our youngest's birth record.

The night she was born I'd been woken up by noises I didn't recognize. Sounds that animals make, or ghosts. I used to sleep through music, smashing glass, collapsing bodies and screaming matches most nights but this time my brain engaged on this unfamiliar sound and woke me.

I followed the sound across our landing and popped my head round the door of our bathroom just in time to hear my mother make that low sound again and see a baby plop from her body on to the floor of the bathroom with a thud.

My eyes went so wide they burned. What on earth . . . ?

So *that's* where babies came from. I'd had no idea. I knew there was a baby in Mum's belly but I kinda figured there'd be a belly button involved in getting it out. This was a whole different story altogether. To say I was surprised doesn't cover it.

Tilly was completely stoned, standing there in the middle of the bathroom with blood everywhere and a baby screaming on the floor between her legs, the grey alien cord sticking to her leg still attached. I did nothing. I just stood there.

'Oh, bloody hell, you've done it now.' John Bean – who was always getting stoned on our sofa – pushed past me in the doorway and picked up the baby with a towel. 'Jesus Christ, Tilly, you've done it now.' She hadn't noticed she was in labour with the strength of the stuff she was taking. And at the last moment she'd felt pressure and so had got up to go to the toilet and birthed the baby.

John Bean wrapped the baby up and handed it to Tilly, who sat down on the toilet. She was spaced and pale. The baby was bright red with an open mouth pulling air in and then there were these huge pauses as it fought to make as much impact as possible with a scream long and hoarse which trembled at the end in a way that pulled on my heart strings. I wanted to take it off my mum because she held it at a strange angle away from her body. But it was still attached. I wondered would she drop it.

My mum said nothing. I hugged the door frame as John Bean passed back and forth. But my dad was stoned too.

I said, 'There's no waking him when he's like that, John.' I was in the know. He patted me on the head.

'I'll call for an ambulance, Tilly, don't move!' he said. 'Do not move!'

There was no chance of her moving. She was out of it. John Bean thundered down the stairs, two at a time.

I stared at my mother, and at this nativity scene from hell, until he came back. As he did, he met my father on the landing, rubbing his face.

'Tilly had the baby in the bathroom,' John Bean said. Then my father skidded into the bathroom where I was sitting now on the edge of the bath, my toes pressed into the side for balance and to avoid the pool of congealing blood and fluid on the floor. Suddenly the hero, like a man on a mission, he was in control. For a minute I believed him.

'Tilly, get your shit together,' my dad said, and lifted the baby up, unwrapping the towel and checking its belly and legs and fingers before swaddling it again and giving it back.

'The rope isn't come out,' I said and then my dad patted me on the head.

The window lit up with the lights of an ambulance; it looked pretty through the patterned privacy glass. And I heard the slow steps of scornful paramedics, saw the eye rolls as they met the scene. Their time and skill were worth more than this.

My mum didn't get comforting words as they lifted her up and brought her down the stairs and into the ambulance. My dad, half dressed, got into the ambulance with her.

'Shouldn't be allowed to have kids,' the driver said as he hoisted his fat belly up into the cab. He looked at me and grimaced in disgust. I pulled my nightie down to my knees and held it there.

When the baby came home my parents were at their worst. The house was a flow of bad. It was a pit of filth, with needles, shoelaces, spoons, ashtrays, bottles, stained carpets, brown ceilings from smoke, a red couch covered in stains of piss and vomit, and scorch marks on everything from hot spoons, dropped cigarettes and hot rocks from joints. People came and went from our house, drugs were dropped in and sold out of it.

Usually, you'd find one of my dad's friends on our couch. It was perfectly normal for me and my brothers to watch Saturday-morning television sitting on the floor with the sleeping body of one of our 'uncles' taking up the couch behind us. Perfectly normal to be prodded in the back and asked to go to get a lighter when they finally woke up. Perfectly normal for them to continue smoking and drinking all day as we came in and out of the house.

There was August, an African immigrant who lived as a Rastafarian, who sat smoking joints with my dad and whose accent was so pleasing to my ear that I would find a reason to hang around and listen, fussing with bits and bobs until I was told to go on. There was Uncle Bob, a huge fat man who lived in the flats. He was not our uncle, though. My dad always said he was an 'uncle by default', but he was nothing to us. And, of course, there was John Bean.

One of my earliest memories of John Bean was from when I was three or four, as I stood wide-eyed at the door of our house. I'd been woken by a crash and a scream, and the noise of my brothers barrelling down the stairs. I followed just in time to see my dad open the front door to a trouserless and bleeding John Bean, who got to his feet and ran out of our gate and over the road towards the flats.

'Jesus Christ.' My dad went to run after him, but immediately hopped backwards like a cat on a hot tin roof, as there were shards of window glass all over the drive.

It seemed that John Bean had, in fact, jumped out of the window of my parents' bedroom and was now running through the streets of Coventry half naked.

'John! Come back!' My dad gave the path a go again but there was no way through. He was barefoot and high, and so he stood there and looked up at the window and out into the night, back and forth a few times as if he was seeing things.

'Bloody hell,' my dad said, and started to laugh.

'Bloody hell,' my brother Michael said, and didn't.

In our childhood photos, John Bean is there, sitting beside my dad with a baby Michael, or James, or me. As well as being there when our youngest was born, he was on the scene when my dad was at his lowest, overdosed and dying. And each time he was the one who called for help.

When I was little I used to associate him with fun. He was really tall, and he would let me hang off his arms and spin me round, taking me off my feet. He was always smiling, and I always looked forward to him coming up the path.

As I got older, and I knew more, I dreaded him. Because John Bean always brought drugs into our house. His visits led to chaos. As I watched John Bean grow gaunt and skinny over the years, and the spliffs in his mouth turned into needles in his arm, I watched my parents follow. He was *that* friend – the one who pulls you back in, the one who can't let you go.

My parents were those people too, don't get me wrong. They were like two drowning kids most of the time, desperately pulling and pushing the other under. But the people around us when we were kids, my parents' friends, were people who cast dark shadows over our lives. And there was one who cast the darkest shadow of all.

My dad was put in prison for selling drugs. Our house felt like a rowing boat in a squall. Nothing was safe. My mother had no money. She had five children to look after but, just as urgent as her children, she had her own addiction to feed as well as my dad's. He needed gear brought into him. She was destitute.

There are no words I can find to describe how low my parents were at that time, or how it felt as a kid to see them struggle, strung out, losing all sense of how to live. Two ghosts in the house, shells of my parents with nothing inside. We were too, us kids, little empty things with no nourishment, no love or food. We would wander around our house surviving, needles lying about, people coming and going.

Then my dad was gone. People knew he wasn't home, so they tried to come in to do drugs in our kitchen. A few times my mum had come home to a kitchen full of addicts doing heroin. So she warned us to keep the doors locked. It became the family policy.

But none of us would have refused one of our 'uncles', and they called all the time when my mum wasn't there. They'd sit on the couch and smoke and we would make them tea, or they'd have cans of beer or cider with them and they'd drink that.

When Uncle Bob arrived one day, I knew something was wrong.

'Have you a new dress?'

He was huffing and sliding sideways, his belt too tight around his fat belly, pulled like a knot in a balloon. He slid down on to the couch, sitting at this awkward angle, sideways on. Drunk. I didn't like the way he was sitting and I didn't like the way he was looking at my legs. I pulled my dress over them and shook my head.

'It's my normal dress,' I told him.

He nodded when I said that and squinted at me again. He huffed and puffed the way fat men always do when their shirts and belts are too tight and they are hot from booze.

Matthew came in and sat down. 'Mum's not here,' he said.

Bob took that in; he lit a cigarette and drew on it deep down into his chest. He shifted again. 'Is Michael here?' he asked.

Matthew said no. Bob fixed a stare on my legs.

Then he said, 'Matthew, do me a favour.' He pushed his back into the couch, stretched to squeeze a hand into his pocket. He pulled out change and flicked a fifty-pence piece to him. Matthew caught it between his hands in a clap.

Uncle Bob said, 'Pop down the shops, mate, will ya? Get some ice creams.'

Matthew hopped up, delighted and smiling. Kids like us rarely had ice creams.

I stood up to go too. Bob shifted, stretched and pulled me back on to the couch. 'Come here, sit beside me.'

His breath smelled sour like our kitchen after a party.

When my dad was in prison my mum usually kept the curtains drawn closed, but on that day they were open. The net curtains were filthy and stained brown from smoke but the sunlight coming through them made a pattern on the red carpet.

When Matthew left I felt really uneasy. Uncle Bob flicked the channels on the TV and drank from a can of beer he was holding. But he kept my hand firmly in his other hand.

'I have to go and tell my friend something,' I said. I twisted my hand in his grip. I wanted to get out of that room, but I didn't want to be rude. He didn't let my hand go.

I didn't like the feel of his sweaty hand holding mine; I didn't like the way he was talking and slurring and the way his sentences trailed off to nothing.

It was confusing because I liked Uncle Bob. He always paid attention to me and Matthew when he came round, and sometimes Matthew got to stay over in his flat down the road, which I was jealous of – I wanted to go too. I couldn't understand why Matthew got to do that, he was always so naughty.

Bob lived with his girlfriend. She was pretty and blonde and wore coloured eyeshadow and leggings. Bob was a thunderous weight of a man, someone who ate and drank and took whatever he wanted, no reserve. Anytime he came into our house my parents would tell us to say hello and be nice to Uncle Bob and not to be rude. So even when he made me so uncomfortable that day, I wanted to be nice to him because I didn't want him to stop giving me attention and only give it to Matthew. I pulled my hand gently, but he kept a hold of it. I left it there. *Don't be rude.*

And so I froze when Bob opened his belt and took down his trousers. Even though the way he did it, very deliberately, frightened me so much, I didn't run or scream. *Don't be rude.*

After, everything was different. I was different.

The little version of me, that little girl who did cartwheels and showed her knickers as she went heels over head on the grass, the little one who laughed with her whole body, the one who chased and fell and jumped and climbed and climbed and climbed, she stayed there in that moment. In the *before*.

And the new me – the guarded one, the devastated un-wilded small thing – she went on as someone else.

Barely seven, forced into performing oral sex by an adult man, that filthy deviant, and when I couldn't do that properly he pushed me back on the couch and raped me.

I did not understand what he was doing.

I did not know what he was doing.

Why was Uncle Bob lying on top of me? What was he doing?

My face pressed into the fat of his chest. I was pinned.

A butterfly on a board.

I did not understand this. Then I did.

So I waited for it to stop.

I wanted to shout out, to howl, but I couldn't inhale, the pressure of his body was too great. I worried Matthew would come back. I worried Matthew was next.

I waited for it to stop.

But it didn't stop, it got worse. The weight of him crushed and suffocated me, my sight dimmed from the lack of oxygen.

I felt deep pain, but I couldn't breathe to cry out.

Tears slid into my ears.

I'm dying.

I think I can pinpoint the moment when the little girl I had been up to that point died and reincarnated into someone else. Under the sticky flab, the sweat, the sour drink-fuelled indulgence of this . . . *animal* who poured his rot over me, crushing my body and my soul.

I switched over. The little one, whose body was a tool of freedom, something she used to move and play and race, she stayed there. This new person, whose body invited this terror, came through.

Eventually Bob rolled away and I was left broken. Not just then but for the rest of time. No matter how much patching I do, no matter how much I attempt to stitch and bring the pieces back together, I can't. Everything was different after that.

When Matthew came home with the ice creams and handed them around, I didn't recognize his face. He had been my best friend but now I didn't know him any more and he didn't really know me. We were strangers. We had been peas in a pod but now that was gone.

A few weeks later my mother brought me with her when we dropped Matthew down to stay with Bob. I hid behind her when he answered the door.

'Don't be rude,' my mother said and pulled me out.

As we left she asked me, 'What's wrong with you? It's not like you to be rude to Uncle Bob.'

So I told her. I knew the word, I'd heard it loads of times before.

'He raped me,' I said. There was a huge sore lump in my throat. A high-pitched ringing appeared in one ear.

My mother, strung out and worn down, stared straight ahead.

'Yeah . . . well, he raped me too,' she said.

I put my hands over my ears.

5

I don't really know how to write about Tilly, my mum. I write the stories about all she said and did and then I feel so protective of her I want to delete it all. And I am angry at her all over again. Maybe I'm afraid that if I describe everything she did, how she neglected and hurt us kids, my love for her simply won't come through and the bad stuff will outweigh it all, and I'll lose her again. Books are so permanent. I've lost my mum so many times and maybe I'm afraid that if I tell it like this, I will lose her for good.

The thing is, I love my mother. Let me start there.

I love my mother.

I always loved my mother. She just didn't know how to love me.

Sylvia Morrissey was called 'Tilly' by her father during her childhood, based on a character in a beloved book. It stuck. She was known as Tilly to everyone. She was born in Coventry to an English mother, Marian, and an Irish father, Mick. Mick was from Athy, Co. Kildare.

Her childhood nickname would give you the impression of a loving home, but her father was an alcoholic who would often beat her with a belt. Her mother, my nanny, had a husband before Mick but was widowed young with four children and those children were taken into care. Even though she remarried, her children were never restored to her, and my mother knew nothing about them until years later one of them arrived at the door. Nanny had told nobody about them, not even her new husband, perhaps because, by all accounts, he was not an easy-going man.

She, however, was the sweetest, most patient lady, with blue misty eyes and grey set hair, and the air around her smelled like Murray Mints. You'd never have imagined she had ever seen a moment of pain or violence when you met her.

My mum told me that often all the money that came in on Friday would be gone on Friday night and a full week would be ahead of them with no food at all. But her mother never complained, never fought with her husband, not even when he beat her child. Not even when he burned her with a poker. She really believed the man was the head of the house. When my parents fought, my nanny always sided with my dad, almost as if she was afraid he would leave my mum. For her, there was no worse fate than being a single woman. Those messages go in.

Tilly was small and beautiful with wide-open eyes that told you what she was thinking with a glance, eyes that told you what state she was in the moment you looked into them. Though she was always drunk or high when I was little, I thought she was cool and different. She was a vision in Indian skirts and coloured runners. She had a wicked sense of humour and a laugh that made everyone else laugh. She loved a party, loved dancing, and she always blared music. And she was addicted to all those things that are bad for women: drugs, drink and one man – my dad.

The story goes that my dad was passing through Coventry and asked Tilly for directions to the train or bus or something. She was eighteen and brave and cheeky, and she gave him directions instead to her flat. The story of how they met was always wrapped up with the words '*and he never left*'.

Thing is, he did, though. When she told him she was pregnant a few months later he ran away back to Ireland. When we were grown up we heard that part of the story – how he panicked and took the boat. He told us that he had left a serious girlfriend in Dublin that summer and didn't know what to do. It could be an excuse. It could be true.

Michael was six months old when my dad finally returned to Coventry, full of guilt and apologies, and Tilly was terribly relieved to see him. Over the years I wondered – I still wonder – if she ever wished he hadn't come back.

Michael was first and then James. Then the rest of us: me, Matthew and the baby.

My mum was always a mess. Her hair was too silky and fine to hold in clips and would end up around her neck in wisps. She used to have me do her hair for her, in a French bun or a plait, but it always fell out. Her clothes were always mismatched: she would start the outfit with good style and intentions but then she would impatiently pull a mismatched hoodie over it all and throw her runners on. Nothing ever fitted across her big chest. Her nose was big too and her earlobes dragged down from the turquoise stones she hung in them. She was untethered, a free bird. Wild at heart.

And she was, of course, an addict, and she was, of course, a bad mother. But even so, I loved her.

Of all of us, maybe my mum suffered the most. My dad went to prison the first time when I was seven. Everything bad that happened, happened then. My mum was addicted to heroin and left to her own devices, left to survive with five children in a shithole house on the frontline of poverty. How on earth could it have gone any other way?

She needed money.

At the end of our road was the church. It's still there, although the grounds seem to be gone now from what I can see on the maps. We used to play there. And it was routine, over the back wall of St Peter's, to taunt and jeer the prostitutes who worked on the other side.

'Twenty pound an hour!' we would shout in unison, popping our heads up over the wall. Then we would fall about laughing so hard. We had no idea what the twenty pounds was about or really what these women were doing. We called out 'sluts' or 'slags' – the worst thing you could call a woman. Sometimes we would jeer them for long enough to get a chase. There was one old one, dyed hair and too much make-up and cheap clothes that fell off her bones. If you booed her she would make a start towards you, and we loved the fright of that. We would run away squealing to hide in the graveyard.

We knew these women were 'bad' and that they deserved to be jeered. The abuse rolled off our tongues because these women deserved it. And if we saw any men who came to use their services we shouted at them and called them 'dirty bastards'. 'Get your leg over!' I shouted at one of them, not really knowing what I was saying.

Then one night I ran down with everyone else and popped my head up to shout, but nothing came out because I was suddenly staring at my own mother standing there with her legs out and lipstick on her mouth. I caught her eye and she stared straight back at me. The world started to crumble under my feet. I ran and ran.

Maybe I'd made a mistake, maybe it wasn't her. I flew home, straight to the kitchen where I knew Michael was. I would tell Michael. He was twelve and he could go down and get her out of it.

'Michael!' I roared his name as I came through the back door. He appeared in the hall.

I told him. Our mum was down at the wall, down by the church. Our mum was down *there*.

He just stared at me. 'I know,' he said. And we stood there looking at each other with the understanding that there was nothing we could do about any of this. Our mum was doing *that* because she needed the money. We got it.

The consequences of my mum not having her gear were horrifying. When you see someone you love sick from drug withdrawals – we called it Jonesing back then – you'd do anything to stop it. When you see them tear at their skin, and vomit for hours, and cry out. When you see them claw the walls and lie on the couch screaming with the muscle aches and the headache of it. They plead with you to make it stop. You'd do anything to get it for them.

Michael could never stand it, not for a minute, when my mother was sick for heroin. None of us could. It drove us all mad to see her like that. It frightened me so much too, because when she was like that I thought she would die.

I just wanted a normal mum. If she was normal then it wouldn't matter if my dad was in prison. I wanted a mum who made dinners and walked us to school. One who called to me from the door to come and get a coat on.

I said all of that out loud and with tears running down my face. Michael just stood there. I knew he wanted that too. We all did. Some of us were just more vocal about it.

I always thought, *If only I could run this.* If I could be the one making the decisions, then it would be okay. That's why I snooped and investigated and kept tabs on everyone. My magical thinking was that if I had all the information I could free us all, eventually. I've had to let that thinking go. I was trying to fix everyone, but that was breaking me.

I didn't sleep at all that night. I was worried about my mum and she wasn't coming back. Then I heard the door go, and Michael's voice and my mum's, and I finally slept.

Years later my mum would often talk about how much shame she carried for what she did. Because society looks down on women who prostitute themselves. But my mother was desperate and alone and forced into that by her circumstances.

I hated it. I hated those men. I knew they were abusing my mother, taking advantage of her addiction. They didn't care that my father was in prison. They didn't care that my mother was doing this because she couldn't cope. It didn't matter to them. They saw a woman in the throes of poverty and addiction and, instead of helping her, they took advantage of her. It made no difference to them that she was ill, worn, thin and upset. They didn't care that she was desperate. She was nothing more than a consumable. A product. Those men abused my mother.

Tilly told me once her motto during that time was 'I just need enough for gear and chips for the kids', and I know even at her lowest point she was trying to look after us.

We were taken into care not long after that.

6

Everyone around us sold drugs to fund their own addiction. People were always calling in, people we knew or friends of friends, to buy drugs and have a cup of tea. They always stayed a while. My mum would pop out of the room and come back with whatever it was, from the hiding place or her bra, and that would be the deal done. Sometimes my dad would tell us in code, 'White coke is coming to collect that,' and he would leave a packet with one of us. By the time I was a teenager we were all selling drugs to cover our own. When it was Es and speed, my whole family would buy them, sell them and take them together.

My dad was arrested after the door of our house was kicked in one morning at six a.m. I was suddenly awake, with policemen screaming at me to get up. They were everywhere in the house, and my dad and mum and brothers were standing facing the wall. During those raids, the police shout at you, right up in your face, every one of them fuelled with pure aggression and anger. I was little at this time and they were truly terrifying. Even now when I watch television and actors play out a raid like that, my skin prickles with adrenaline and I am frightened.

There was this policeman, Phil Parker, and he was like the devil to me, a real old-school villain. When we saw him – and he was always around our way – we ran. He used to pull up and search my brother Michael. Just for something to do, it seemed, because he never found anything. I suppose it was a method of intimidating my dad, a message to say we know what's going on in your house. But that was the most unfair thing, because when my brother Michael was pulled up, rammed against a wall and searched, he was only a kid. And he was frightened of those men. And he was frightened of my dad, because when he told him what had happened my dad's first words would be, 'I hope you said nothing.'

Those police didn't see us kids as victims, not at all. They saw us as vermin, in the same way a farmer might see a den of fox cubs. And they treated us like that, like we were animals.

I remember Phil Parker being in our house during one of those raids: I was sitting on the floor and I was crying, and he lifted a pair of my mum's underwear off the pile on the chair and held them up to me. The gusset was stained.

'Look at that,' he said, and he stretched them out. 'Your mother is a dirty tramp, the state of this.'

He flung the underwear at me then, and I flinched when

they landed right by me. My parents told me over and over again never to trust the police. They warned us never to ask them anything, not for help, nothing. And here they were, in our house, dragging my dad in his underwear out of his bed, pushing my twelve-year-old brother up against the wall and screaming in his ears. Throwing my mother's underwear at her seven-year-old daughter.

My parents were right.

We would go as a family down to the prison to see my dad and to give him drugs. We went every two weeks. One of us kids would have to keep the drugs in our underwear, because my mum would be searched by the prison officers on the way in, whereas we were just patted down. When I say my mother would be searched, I mean she was assaulted. Every visit. The prison officers felt her body and if she resisted they would threaten her.

'Tilly, do you want this visit cancelled?' one of them said. She was so thin then, and like a ghost, holding me by the hand.

My brother James pushed his chest out, shifted on his feet like a man about to fight. He was small and wiry then, undernourished, but so *so* brave. My heart was pounding at the sight of it all, and because I had a bag of gear wrapped tight in cling film and tucked into the crease of my body, in my knickers.

'Stop it,' my mum said, but the prison officer took his

time anyway. Like the police, they didn't see us as 'children' that you should be appropriate around. We were the pups of scum as far as they saw it, and so afforded no dignity or respect at all.

We saw my dad then, and he looked great. Fed well, tanned in his prison striped shirt and jeans, he kissed my mother and swallowed the small packet she passed him with her tongue. It was a routine. We would arrive in the prison, my mum would retrieve the packet from me and then keep it in her mouth until she saw my dad.

My mum — and our situation — got worse and worse the longer my dad was gone. Tilly was so strung out, so lost, that she was barely there and the worst thing about it was that the baby — now a toddler — was wandering around in the middle of it all, most of the time in a soiled nappy. Me and my brothers, we were the barest of caretakers.

Things came to a head and the baby ended up in hospital, badly burned. That day my mum was in a terrible mood. I'd brought the cigarette lighter up to her in bed and gone back downstairs. Around an hour later the toy box in the boys' room was on fire, just smouldering. It took ages for us to put it out. I didn't have a clue how it started but Mum blamed me. She was convinced I had done it. So I was in the bad books.

Later, around teatime, my mum was back in bed and

she called down to bring her a cup of tea. While I was making the tea, the baby was asking for some too.

'Boppy tea,' she said, pulling at my hand.

'Stop,' I said. I wanted to get Mum her tea.

'Boppy tea,' she said again, showing me the empty bottle and then grabbing it with her teeth and pulling the teat out.

'If you break it there'll be no boppy,' I said, taking the bottle off her and placing it on the counter out of reach.

The kettle was heavy and I had to lift it up higher than my own head to pour the hot water into the cup. I added the milk and sugar, stirred it how my mum liked it, and I left the room and went up the stairs as quick as I could without spilling any, holding the handle and trying not to let the scalding cup press against my knuckles. Last time it had I'd dropped it.

My mum had two hands out to take it when I came into the room.

'Thanks,' she said.

From the kitchen the baby let out a scream and the scream kept going.

I knew instantly what had happened. I'd left the kettle over beside the fridge, with the cord hanging down. In my rush to get the tea to my mum, I hadn't put it back. The baby had pulled down the kettle full of boiling water. I knew it.

I was terrified. I backed out of the room as my mother

jumped up, cursing. As she ran down the stairs, I ran into the bathroom and crouched down in the corner, the plastic side of the bath sticky against my bare shoulders.

The baby was burned.

The hullabaloo downstairs went on and on. An ambulance came. I stayed curled up in the bathroom until it was bedtime and then I crept into my room.

The baby was gone for weeks. I was so sorry.

It was to be the story of the baby's life, being away from us. She'd spent her first few months in hospital, and then was in hospital again this time. And when all of us were taken into care, she wasn't with us. She was given to a foster family, and we didn't see her for the entire time until we were given back to my mum. The connect was disrupted.

And when we were all back together, I was heading into my early teens and didn't want a bar of her. She was so much younger than I was, she needed so much more than I knew how to give her. She followed me around and I told her to go away. I wish I could go back and change that, pick her up and take her off to make daisy chains in the back yard. Or let her join in my dance routines or just talk to her.

That's what I'm sorry for. If I'm honest.

I'm sorry for all of it. What we went through, what we saw, what we learned. It never should have been that way. Knowing what I know now, about the early years, I wish

I could have been a better sister to that baby. But we were all surviving, every one of us. And we can't take it back.

My mother told me with stares that the burn was my fault, every time my sister was getting dressed or undressed and I saw the rippling pink scar where the water hit her, but I know it wasn't.

I shouldn't have been making tea, the baby shouldn't have been in the kitchen. My mother shouldn't have been lying in bed. I knew that then, when it happened, I knew it wasn't my fault. All of that was my mum's fault.

I was still going to Brownies every week even though things were crazy at home with my dad in prison. School and Brownies were the two things that were getting me through. I liked anything organized and in Brownies I loved the uniform. It meant I blended in. I was just like the other girls, no difference at all. I have always found fuel in achievements – anything where I could follow steps and receive praise was for me. In Brownies I listened to instructions, learned to sew and do little tasks to earn badges. I liked to sing as loud as I could and clap my hands and have fun. All the little girls at St Peter's Brownies in Hillfields needed things like that to get us through the week. I never missed it. I always made my own way to and from Brownies.

And so I knew something was up as soon as I saw my older brothers waiting outside to collect me.

Their eyes were red.

'We're going into care,' my brother James said. They both started crying so I did too, even though I didn't really know what was happening or what *care* was, not exactly. But I knew it was bad.

'Baldy next door grassed on Mum for staying out,' James said. Michael balled up his fists when James said that.

We all hated Baldy next door. He always stretched his neck to peer as far as he could into our house whenever he could, sometimes sweeping his drive for hours just in case we would come or go and he could get a glimpse of life inside.

My mum had left us instructions on how to pretend she was at home, but he had seen through it and called the police. In fairness, she had left us all there with the baby for more than twenty-four hours.

That walk home was the longest of my life. 'Care' was the thing my parents feared most, along with 'losing our money' and 'getting our house taken off us'. It was what they screamed at each other when they fought and what they bargained with in attempts to get the other clean.

As we walked up our road, I watched a strange lady exit our house with the baby in her arms. She got into a taxi and it left. Michael started crying so hard then. When we went inside our house I saw another lady sitting there. I knew her, she was one of many ladies in flowery dresses who called to our house with clipboards and asked my mum questions. A social worker. This one was sitting at our table, where she had pushed aside some of the piles of dirty washing, charity shop books and empty cans to create a little space for her cup of tea. Two policemen stood outside the back door.

The way the lady smiled at me when I came in put me on my guard. She looked friendly but she wasn't being friendly. I looked around and said, 'Where did our baby go?'

'Your little sister is going to stay with a family,' the social worker said, and she gently clapped hands into the tops of her legs when she said it. Like the Brown Owl would when you were about to do something fun at Brownies.

Something wasn't right here.

'Why?' I said.

'Mum needs a break,' she said. 'I think we all need a little break.'

A break? Like a holiday? My mum was going on holiday? Why could we not all go? What was this?

The social worker said then that there was a taxi outside now and we were to go and get into it. We did. And we all started crying.

'They're taking us to the children's home,' Michael said as if we were on our way to hell. He looked out of the back window, desperate. I could see his mind racing behind his eyes when he turned to me and Matthew, who were sitting together in the corner of the cab's back seat, and he said, 'Do not say one word here, okay?'

We nodded, agreed. Not one word.

'Don't say one word, tell them nothing.' James echoed our older brother and he even pointed in our faces, first Matthew, then me, with the same urgency we were used to from our parents when they used the same words.

James was one of those kids who oozed cool. He slicked his hair and smoked by the age of ten. He had a swagger, my brother, like he knew where he was going. And he was popular for it. He had cool friends who I adored, but he never let me play. I was the little sister, the pest.

But I had one power over him, and I used it – my gender. I remember using that against him so many times. It was a small advantage that didn't last long. He had these toy soldiers I loved. A big bucket of them, all in different poses; they were good quality and satisfying to hold and play with. 'If you don't give them to me, I'll tell Dad you hit me,' I hissed once.

I remember the injustice written all over his face. My dad had a low moral code, but he never hit women. And so, in our house, that was a cardinal rule and I used it over and over again. My dad kept a wooden paddle down by the TV and he would take it out and use it to punish my brothers if they stepped out of line. Nobody was ever sure where the line was drawn. But we all knew that hitting girls was well over it.

'I'll say you're lying,' James said but he knew he was finished. He pressed his lips together, the dimples on the tops of his cheeks appearing when he did.

I knew it too. 'Daaaaaad!' I called out.

James shoved the tub of soldiers into my hands.

He uncrossed his legs, resigned. Then he leaned over and fished a half-smoked cigarette out of the huge salt stone that was used as an ashtray in our living room. It was one of those rose-coloured mineral licks for cattle that my dad had found in a field years before and lugged home with him.

'I'm going out,' James said. He gave me the finger and left. He knew how to hurt me too.

I remember one time James ran away. He had been grounded, I think, and a match was on so he left the house anyway and a night passed. We all went out looking for him and I found his jacket stuffed in a bush – it was unmistakable – and convinced myself the wet patch on it was blood and he'd been kidnapped and murdered. At that time kids were always being told horror stories about men in vans.

I'd never felt like that before, terror by proxy. The thought of my brother being hurt by someone, it was awful. My heart went cold and I felt as though I couldn't breathe. I hung on to his jacket and shouted his name until I was hoarse.

James told me later he had been watching from the top of the Coventry Football Club Community Centre as we all searched and called out his name. He decided he might as well be hanged for a sheep as a lamb, came home eventually and walked in the door as if he had just walked out of it.

My relief in seeing him back didn't last long. We were fighting again in no time as siblings do. Years later, when he told me about the jacket, he told me how it was him who set the fire in the toy box too. To get me back for the paddle.

We laugh now, but when you think of it – all of it – it's really sad. James had a swagger that said he knew where he was going. Thing is, he was as lost as any of us.

Keresley Grange looked like a mansion from a movie when we first pulled up outside. It is a school now, I believe. That's a good thing. It was dark and the lights inside glowed yellow. The night sky was dark blue and the roof was pitched against it, a Victorian skyline, a fairy-tale house. I stopped crying.

The doors of the Grange opened and a man appeared. He was tall and had glasses on and a plaid shirt that he had rolled up to his elbows. He called out cheerily in a

West Country accent that you couldn't be afraid of if you tried, 'Well, hello, O'Sullivans!' and waved.

I waved back, and Michael hit me with dagger eyes.

We were ushered in to meet a line of other staff who all patted us on our heads and greeted us warmly, and then the man brought us through a glass door into the foyer. There were two phones on the wall, encased in those plastic hoods to muffle your conversation. There was a wide bending staircase up to a landing with rooms off it.

'Do not tell them nothing,' Michael kept hissing over and over. 'Not one thing, do not tell them one thing, we will be out of here tomorrow.'

We nodded solemnly every time he said it. We were the resistance.

We went up the stairs then, following the man who introduced himself as Tim. Tim showed us the bathrooms with their clean corners and white towels on hooks. There was toilet roll with flowers on it in the cubicles.

A lady came and told me her name was Grace – 'Yes, Katriona, just like in the song' – and then she took my hand and showed me a small room with an empty bed along the wall. Opposite that was another bed with a girl in it. She turned her head on the pillow and looked at me.

'Katriona,' my guide said, 'this is where you're going to sleep, just for now, okay?'

I wasn't sure. 'I want to stay with Matthew,' I said. But the lady shook her head and patted the empty bed. She cooed at the other little girl, warned her that she was going to turn on the light and did so. Then she lifted a bag that was hanging from my bed and took out of it a new pair of pyjamas and handed them to me. There were tags on them.

'Go have a wash up,' she said, 'have a nice bath if you want to, and then pop these on.' She pointed me out of the door to the loo and switched off the light again.

I crossed paths with Matthew on my way back. He was wearing new pyjamas too and had his hair brushed.

What was this place?

I cried that night, exhausted and overwhelmed. I wanted to be in the same room as my brothers. The lady had brushed my hair and patted my head and helped me into bed and tucked me in. And I cried the whole time. Which I felt terrible about, because I liked the new pyjamas and the fresh bed, and the hot milk they gave me. I liked it so much I was even wondering how I could sabotage the plans Michael had to get us home. In our house, beds were full of springs and you had to curl yourself into knots to avoid them. In our house, nobody had pyjamas or clean sheets. In our house, towels were always wet and smelly, and there were no soft blankets, and pillows were stained and hard. Nobody tucked you in there or gave you hot milk.

The childcare worker, Tim, who had greeted us, popped his head around the door – probably to see if everyone was asleep – and saw that I was crying, so he sat down at the end of my bed for a bit. The other child was awake too and he told us a little story about a caterpillar. Then he told me not to worry and, as he closed the door, he said, 'Night night, kids,' like you'd hear parents say in the movies.

I slept a bit. I knew it was time to get up when I could hear the sounds of the house coming awake, and people being busy. The other little girl was still asleep. I sat up and saw at the end of my bed a new tracksuit with tags on, new pants, socks and a T-shirt with all different patterns on it. They were for me.

The other little girl woke and sat up. She rubbed her face a few times and yawned.

'Do we still go to school?' I asked her.

'Don't really know about you,' she said, 'but I do.'

I followed that little girl in getting dressed and washed and then downstairs where we went into a large room with round tables all set up with knives and forks and spoons. Under the windows there were long tables and on those were boxes of cereals, different kinds, and jugs of milk, and toast in piles with baskets full of jams and butter. There was a hot tureen with porridge. A man put a plate down with a cover on it. I lifted it and there were sausages under it. My eyes nearly fell out of my head.

My brothers sat on hunger strike to one side. I looked at them. I looked at that table. I looked at my brothers again. Michael shook his head slowly, a warning. Then I saw the Marmite.

Well, I marched over to that table and helped myself. I took toast and sausages and butter and Marmite. I took a bowl and filled it with Rice Krispies and put sugar on it. Then I marched myself to a table by myself, defiant, and sat down and ate every single bit of it. I heaped my spoon with cereal and stuffed my mouth with it. I ignored the weight of Michael's stare.

My feet swung under my chair in the rhythm of a child getting fed, and as I chewed the sausages, I closed my eyes. This place was heaven.

'Stop looking so happy.' I was poked back to the room. It was James. He whispered the words out of the corner of his mouth. Matthew made a run for the door and was returned to his seat by the staff. He kicked at them and told them to get their hands off.

I shrugged and spooned the food into me for fear he would knock it off the table. I was a turncoat. I didn't care.

Walking into school, arriving there by taxi, with new clothes, clean hair and a fresh body, I felt like I had won the lottery. Even my school bag was new. The girls in my class stared at me when I came in.

'Where'd you get that tracksuit, Katriona?' one asked me.

'None of your business,' I said.

'Her mum probably stole it,' I heard another one of

them say. I didn't care much. I was too busy thinking about what was for dinner at the children's home that night.

I had such a sense of safety there, away from our house where things were wild and unpredictable, where I was fed to the lions by my parents who put their addictions before everything else, where I was starved and cold and unloved. I wanted these hot dinners. I wanted these clean clothes. I wanted the stories at bedtime.

At night we would sit, all of us in the care home, around these round tables and they would bring us good nutritious dinners and glasses of milk and a pudding.

'What is this?' I said to the dinner lady as she brought me a second helping. She told me, 'Calves' tongue,' and I noticed another child gurn at the thought. She put her fork down and pushed her plate away. I didn't give a shit; it was the nicest thing I had ever eaten. The spoon couldn't go fast enough into my mouth. It's still to this day the best meal of my life.

Michael pinched me really hard. 'Stop looking so happy, Kat, Jesus Christ.'

That night after dinner they told us we could ring our mum. I didn't want to.

James gave me such a stare when I refused, so I gave her a few words, a 'Hi, Mum, it's me' before I stood away. They were all crowded around the receiver, standing in this little cubby in the foyer, with a member of staff sitting a bit away in the hall. I remember backing off and wanting the staff to see that. I wanted it to be noted, recorded, that I was not rushing to talk to my mum. I could play *this* system – I wanted to stay.

Later, I'd refuse to go on access visits; I remember crying and saying I didn't want to. I just wanted peace, I wanted safety and the rights to my own body. My mum didn't provide that. Our life with her was full of mayhem and pain.

Eventually our case made it to court, and my mum got us back. I told the court I didn't want to go home, but I was sent back anyway. And when we were dropped off at the house by the black cab and we went in, my mother was strung out and starving and the house was a filthy cesspit, and there was nothing clean or new and everything was worse than we had left it and I was devastated.

And word spread that we were home. Bob came round again.

We must have been at the children's home for six months, and for that whole time I was happy there. My brothers, however, were not. This is the difference between them and me, I think, summed up. They wanted to be at our home, out of loyalty and a sense of belonging. The underclasses have a culture of sticking with your own that runs deep. But I wanted better because I felt, I really felt, I deserved better than what we were given.

It's something my brothers say to me even now: *You think you're better than what we come from, don't you?*

The truth is, yes. It was my answer then and it's the same now: I do think that.

But they have one thing wrong. I don't think I'm the only one. Every single one of us O'Sullivans is better than what we came from. We are clever, funny, spirited people. We deserved more.

I didn't get my wish to stay in Keresley Grange, and we were signed out of supervision completely three years later. The report said:

> This family show a very strong emotional attachment to one another and although the children have been exposed to their parents' 'lifestyle' they show very few signs of disturbance. This is a family that will experience one crisis after another by virtue of their unconventional behaviour but appear to have the resources to override any difficulties and maintain a reasonable family life.
>
> Given the above factors 1) their capabilities to manage their own lives and 2) expiry of the supervision orders 3) change of area and 4) probation involvement it would appear that our intervention is no longer necessary or required.

I don't know what to say about the social workers who dealt with us because even now, with many years of experience and my education in psychology, I don't know what to make of them.

I know it's not part of the normal course of a child-hood to have an assigned social worker, but for us it was as normal as day. Adults, usually middle-class women and men working for the social services, were in our lives as standard. There were lots of them and they were all the same, the civil-servant type, frowning and purs-ing their mouths as if you were a bad stain. Signing on to the dole, we met with people like that; going down to the council office, we met with people like that; in the classroom, our teachers were people like that.

Them and us.

You could tell them on sight, which side of the sys-tem they were on. You'd know by the way someone moved if they were to be trusted or if you were to put on a show. We were trained from birth to 'say nothing' to these people. We knew they had power, to take our money, our house, us kids.

When we were in care, they brought me to the doc-tor for cystitis, a condition that is sometimes a sign of child sexual abuse, and a doctor examined me for that reason. The reports of that examination went missing and were not part of the court proceedings to return us to our mother. The social worker's report noted that it was my mum who asked them to do that examination.

I should never have been returned to that house. Not

without finding out who it was that was abusing me. Those social workers had to have known that was happening.

It was like they destined us for misery. Those who were there to help thought we were so far gone that we didn't deserve more than the lot we had. They just ticked the boxes and did the bare minimum. Those paid by the state to ensure the safety and well-being of children, didn't. They had ample evidence that we weren't safe and they ignored it. They sent me home to starve and stink. They sent me home to be abused.

I know my parents let us down, significantly. The blame is with them. Of course it is. But the world around us let us down too, and in a way that is worse. Because my parents were drug addicts and that is how it all got so bad and messed up. But the people of the world around us – the police, the teachers, the social workers – they were untrustworthy. They pushed us into the corner and frightened us. How could we have grown up to do anything else but bite them back?

My parents let me down but so did the world. And the world was where I had to live.

7

Being a poor kid, growing up in a home that is unstable and surrounded by people who are unpredictable, you never know how a day will go or what's going to happen next. Most of the time it feels like you're living under a blanket of cloud, but every so often the sun breaks through. These pockets of sunshine, they keep you warm. That's how the poor live.

For almost a year after my dad got out of prison it seemed like one pocket of sunshine after another. He came home a few months before Christmas. The first thing he did was go down to the flats and beat Bob to within an inch of his life. He was off drugs and he was furious. He wouldn't speak to any of the friends he had in Hillfields. The men he had asked to keep an eye out for Tilly and us had let him down, abused her and abused me.

He started knocking around with this younger guy, Keith, who had a flashy car and a glamorous girlfriend. Those two would come round all the time, always with posh bottles of wine and sweets for us kids. Keith told my mum he had a spot for my dad, a real job, and everything changed. 'No looking back now, Tilly,' my dad kept saying when they talked about it.

And it seemed there was no looking back. We didn't know ourselves. My dad wore a suit and left the house in the morning, going in the car with Keith, and then he would come back in the evening. Everything was good, but my dad was still angry and he just wanted to get my mum, and me, away from Hillfields. So first we moved from Vine Street to Stoney Stanton Road, a few kilometres away. Later, we would move again, to Birmingham.

My dad said the good fortune was down to me. He said I'd started this train of luck by winning the raffle at school just after his release. I was nine. Everyone in school had been given a ticket and the prize – a larger-than-life portrait of the king of pop, Michael Jackson, which someone had donated – was displayed at the top of the room. We all sat in rows, waiting, and a teacher did a drum roll with his tongue while the head teacher fumbled in the box of tickets, making a big show of swishing her hand around.

'Number sixty-two,' she called out. I didn't react at first. I was sitting there holding my little green ticket, in a space just behind everyone else.

'Number sixty-two! Six-two!' the head teacher called again. The little girl in front of me leaned left and right, checking everyone's tickets, then she turned round and looked at mine.

'That's your one,' she said, and I stared at it.

I read the six and the two. My hand went straight up.

A nearby teacher crossed the floor and checked. 'Well done,' she said, ushering me to my feet. 'You won.'

I passed by my teacher, Mrs Smythe. With her black wiry hair that looked like a witch's hat, she was straight out of a Roald Dahl novel. The nose she looked down at me from strained to meet her pointy chin, and she pulled her mouth down at the corners and folded her arms and said loudly to the teacher next to her, 'Wouldn't have thought you'd hang paintings in a dustbin.'

I felt the sting of her disdain. School had been a sanctuary for the first two years, but the last two – with this harridan – were a cruel trap. She had made my life worse.

'Why have you no pen? Again?' she used to say to me week-in week-out. It was a constant battle. I always shrugged and said I forgot.

I didn't have a pen, Mrs Smythe, you horrible cow, because my parents were junkies and my family was a shambles and there were no pens in my house and I had no money to buy one. Oh, and the ones I robbed from your desk to avoid this tiresome conversation were taken out of my bag and used as pipes by my parents.

She picked on me. She asked me the same questions again and again. Her attitude trickled down, and my classmates treated me just the same.

'Oh, Katriona doesn't have her pen again, Miss,' they told on me.

Mrs Smythe always banged the table, with this pursed mouth and dagger eyes, a fat ball of frustration and anger that outweighed the actual problem being presented. 'I am sick and tired of you, Katriona O'Sullivan.'

You don't say.

Mrs Smythe was something like a thunderstorm. In the middle of class she would erupt, breaking through the noise of scratching pens working out sums on paper, that gentle quiet of students, with a scream. Someone's name, usually mine.

'Katriona O'Sullivan!'

Her voice was like a siren in your sleep, it shocked your body and made your adrenaline spike. I'd snap my head up from my work or from a book – my one joy – and see her coming for me in her flowery dress, her arms straight down by her side with fists balled.

'What is this?' She would slam whatever it was down on the table, or snapped whatever it was up, and stand ranting in her fit of rage until I was exhausted. She called me up to her desk, to do whatever the minimum required interaction was with her students, to do spellings or tables or whatever, and she would make this face like she had caught a bad smell as I came closer. She would always push me back, or back up her chair, and turn her face away with the unmistakable expression of someone repulsed.

If I had a pen, it was the wrong colour; if I had a

pencil, it should have been a pen. If I had no pen, I was the worst person in the world.

'Go to the head and tell her you've no pen again, so you can't be in my class,' she said.

But I'd never go, I'd hang around the toilets or go home. A student missing. But she never cared about that. She never looked for me.

When I was small I read so much. I'm pretty sure I was reading before I went to school and even now I am never without a book. My mum always got piles of them from the charity shop for my dad, and we read those too. Everyone in our house read. And in school we had a whole library. I think I read every novel in it in the first four or five years of school. I loved *The BFG*. I read *Matilda* too. The nights I read *The BFG*, I stared at my own bedroom window, wishing he would come get me; the nights I read *Matilda*, I dreamed of going to live with a lovely teacher. Reading about other kids in trouble gave me hope: it told me I was not the only one; it showed me that I could find my way.

'You're a great reader, Katriona,' the teacher in charge of the library would tell me as she signed out another book for me.

And before Mrs Smythe's class I loved to read aloud; it was something that gave me huge self-esteem. Mrs Arkinson had always told me I was a wonderful reader and whenever she called on me to stand up and read to the class I buzzed with pride. When I read I felt smart and capable.

After two years in Mrs Smythe's class I never wanted to read out loud again. She would stop me, pretending I had gone wrong when I hadn't. She halted my progress and did it with venom, correcting mistakes I hadn't made, gaslighting me, pushing me over the edge.

'Oh dear,' she would say and give this look of utter contempt, 'can't you get anything right?'

At first, horrified by this sudden downturn in my abilities, I tried to improve, but eventually I just let it go. I shrugged it off. I stopped putting my hand up, stopped wanting to take part, stopped loving reading at all.

But she would choose me anyway: 'Katriona O'Sullivan, read for the class.' She picked and picked me to pieces. The truth of it is that she was a bully, and she used her power to strip me bare until I was gone. She intimidated me at school. I thought I would never get away from her. And when they assigned me to her classroom again for a second year I started to mitch every single day. I hated school because of her. I hated her. I was so relieved the following September when I was finally out of that witch's clutches.

So when she made the remark about the dustbin she took the win away. The kids nearest her giggled when she said it and looked at me.

My cheeks went hot and I pulled my sleeves down and held on to them with my fingers. I put my head down, walking the green mile to collect my prize. I had been excited when I won, but now, exposed by Mrs Smythe, it felt like an execution.

I was dirty and belonged in a dustbin and it felt like everybody knew that. I didn't want to go up but everyone was clapping. All I could hear was those words; the whole school thought I was trash. I wanted to cry.

They handed the painting to me.

'Well done, Katriona,' the head said.

I carried it back down and I could hardly see over it. Matthew helped me wrap it in black plastic bags afterwards and we lugged it home between us.

Every time I looked at that painting I was reminded of what Mrs Smythe had said. That horrible snob, that cruel cow. In the years I had the misfortune of knowing her she taught me what is fair and what is not. So now, a teacher myself, I never ask my students why they don't have a pen. There is always a jar of pens by the door in my classroom.

We all liked the new house. It was clean and had no bad memories. I could sit on the couch there and not think about *it*. I got bunk beds in my room, and the baby was back with us and she slept underneath. I would hear her sucking on her bottle when I was reading in the lamplight that came through the window from the street. There were no drugs in our house on Stoney Stanton Road, nobody calling to buy anything, no hidden bags of gear under the new carpet.

On the run-up to Christmas that year, we all knew there would be presents from the way my dad was talking and we were so excited. We weren't used to that. We were kids who didn't believe in Santa. We were those kids you don't want around yours in the lead-up to Christmas, the ones who tell other kids there is no such thing. We knew there wasn't because of all the kids in the world, if there was a Santa, he would have come to us. There is something so sad about that.

Recently I was sitting in a cafe having breakfast with my two younger sons and I texted my brother James and asked him if he had ever believed in Santa. He replied with a strong *NO!* and I burst into tears. I'd forgotten about the time, before my dad went into prison, when things were really bad, that James got a bike on Christmas morning and he was delighted. My dad sold it the next day for money for gear.

But that Christmas morning, at the end of 1986, after a night of tossing and turning with excitement, we all flew downstairs because we knew we would get presents, and there were so many I could barely breathe at the sight of the scene under the tree.

My brothers had got a TV between them, and Matthew

got a bike. I got a white 'Rasta Blaster', which was a double-cassette ghetto blaster. I was delighted. I loved singing, and this had a feature to record your own voice while playing the song. It was brilliant.

Everything was so good at that time. My dad had got my mum a fancy shagpile carpet in the sitting room, and we had to take our shoes off coming into the house. We were all dressed well. The fridge had food in it. There was cereal and yoghurts and sweets on Fridays. My dad even got a new car.

And to cap it all, our team, Coventry, won the FA Cup Final. I'll never forget that day, 16 May 1987. In our house in the tiny sitting room we all crowded around the TV as my hero, Brian Kilcline, and his teammates ran on to the pitch. The run-up to this final had been dramatic, and there were commemorative songs and merchandise for weeks beforehand. The crowds in Wembley were huge, and we roared along.

My parents were drinking cans and smoking, and we were all together, all seven of us, with the door closed. Nobody was causing trouble, nobody was in trouble, nobody was sick. It was wonderful.

We made bets on the outcome. I said 3–2 and was laughed out of the room. 'You're mad,' James said and clicked his fingers at me. There were free kicks and goals disallowed, and the game had us on edge. So we all started arguing, nothing serious or negative, just good-humoured banter, like any normal family, back and forth about the referee and his decisions, as if we knew it all.

And when it went to extra time at 2–2, I was in with a shot of winning that bet. We were all tense and the room went quiet. 'We could lose this,' my dad said.

I knew, and my brothers knew, that if we lost the match there was a chance we would lose everything. My dad never dealt well with defeat. I thought about the times before, when his team had lost, and he would leave the house and not come back.

The tension was more than just about football. And so, when Tottenham scored an own goal, the ball bouncing off Gary Mabbutt's knee and through the posts, my house took off. It burst at the seams and exploded outwards with the excitement and love that had been held hostage by that match. It was okay; we were okay.

My dad was picking us up, swinging us round – he was on fire. He hugged and kissed my mum. My cheeks hurt from smiling. Then my dad piled us into the car and drove us into the city centre with the windows down. The pubs had already spilled into the streets in celebration, and people were dancing and hugging. It was a party. We saw people we knew and my dad honked the horn, slowing down so we could yell out of the window.

On the drive back he put on his tapes and we all sang

along. I felt like things were better. Everything was going to be okay.

That year, 1987, was the best of my life.

'Kids, what do you think about all of us going on a holiday?' The words sounded like another language coming out of my dad's mouth. We had never been on holiday, just over to Ireland once or twice to see Grandad and Granny in Dublin. He leaned back against the door frame.

'You don't want to go?' he said, teasing us.

We jumped up – of course we wanted to go! Where were we going? How long for? He told us Keith and Sandra were coming too. I thought that was exciting. I loved Keith and Sandra. Everything about them was so shiny. They were glamorous.

Mablethorpe was a holiday park – like Butlin's – on the coast of Lincolnshire. We drove there, singing and arguing all the way. We had new clothes and suitcases and cool runners. We were going to take over, we told each other.

We were assigned to two small caravans that were facing one another. We dropped everything off and my parents headed straight to the bar. They were clean then, no drugging, just drinking.

We kids raced around, checking the place out. We found the beach and chased each other across the sand,

we found the playground and the pool hall and the res-
taurant with the all-you-can-eat buffet. We discovered a
field full of horses and pulled grass up in clumps to feed
them, petting their velvet noses and telling each other
everything we knew about them. We argued over things,
ran around. We were excited, busy and free.

'I'm entering it,' I said as soon as I saw the poster go
up for the singing competition. The prize was another
week at Mablethorpe. I knew what I would sing and I
knew what I would wear. I'd been recording myself on
the Rasta Blaster for months now. I knew it would be a
walk in the park.

'You should,' said James, high off the elation of winning the pool competition the night before.

This was our year. We were in full bloom. We were on
the up. Everything we touched turned to gold.

That night I took to the stage dressed in a little green-
striped top and skirt my mum had bought in C&A.
Sandra had done my make-up. I was a five-foot-high
material girl who held that microphone like a seasoned
bar singer. And I won.

I remember the crowd of my family, clapping and
cheering. The way my dad and Michael did an Irish jig,
holding elbows, and James whistled with his fingers
in his mouth. I never felt pride like it. I'd won more
of this, we could have more of this, and it was down
to me.

As we drove back for a second week at Mablethorpe a month later I felt brilliant. The radio was on, music we all knew. We sang along. My mum had the window down, the rushing air blowing the hair back from her face. She was smiling and singing as loud as she could.

It was the best year. It was the dream life. But it was all a lie.

I knew Sandra had told my mum something bad from the way my mother was drinking her beer. She was holding the can in the way she did when her mind was racing. Her eyes were focused on a spot on the ceiling of the caravan and she just stared at it.

Then she put the can down, lifted the box of Bensons off the table and pulled one out, put it in her mouth and lit it with the exaggerated moves of an angry woman.

'Doing cards,' she said, 'those bastards.'

'Tilly, I thought you knew,' Sandra said.

'No. I didn't know,' my mum said. She stretched her neck and pursed her mouth up. She drank more.

My heart hit the floor. 'Doing cards' was what my dad did when he had other people's credit cards. My dad would fill trolleys in B&Q or Dixons with things he could sell and paid for them with stolen cards. You signed for credit in those days, and the cashier would put the card into this metal stamp machine and run it back and forth to get a carbon print of the card which they would have you sign. If you went over a certain amount they'd call the credit card company for clearance.

Sometimes it would go pear-shaped at the till and we always knew to go ahead, push the trolley outside and hide it. That was the go-to plan B every time. So when the cashier began to fuss, lifting the phone to call the credit card company, I would just go ahead. And once I got to the exit I would run with the trolley as far as I could and hide it. One time I was racing away with the trolley, while over my shoulder I could see my dad running the other way, followed by security guards. Then they spotted me and one of them split off with a loud 'Hey, you!' I found a bush against the wall of an alley, abandoned the trolley and hid in it, so I lost them and they ran back after my dad instead.

When the coast was clear I ventured out from my hiding place and found my dad down the way, sitting on a kerb out of breath.

'Bastards,' he said. 'Trolley gone?'

I nodded.

Petty fraud was part of our lives. I never thought much about it. How my parents paid for things was irrelevant to me. It was other people's cash or other people's cards one way or another. But I knew he could get into real trouble if he was caught.

My mum and Sandra had been talking all evening. In the caravan there were built-in sofas with these little fold-out tables and they were sitting across from one another. I had been listening to their conversation the whole time, sitting on the floor by the open door of the caravan, playing on the steps as a cover for keeping my ear open. I always eavesdropped. Being in the know gave me a sense of safety.

So far, I knew that Keith had done something – maybe flirted or danced with another woman – and Sandra had been crying over that. My mum thought that Sandra could get any man she wanted. My mum thought Keith didn't deserve her. Sandra said she didn't want another man and whispered something in my mum's ear that made my mum laugh for ages and call Sandra a dirty bitch and then a fool.

'You tell him when he gets back, Tilly,' Sandra said. 'Be mean to him – he'll be nicer to me if he thinks you're annoyed at him.'

'He won't care what I think,' my mum said.

'He will, Tilly, just be mean to him . . . for me.' Sandra tipped her can off my mum's can. Then she said, 'They actually think they're real businessmen the way they strut around here in those suits.' She got my mum's attention. 'They looked like total fools last week in those priests' costumes. I nearly died when Keith came in looking like that.'

My mum's head whipped round.

Sandra went on, 'I said, "Does this mean I'm a nun?"'

And she cackled and tipped her can off my mum's again. Then she shook her head and laughed some more and drank her beer.

My mum was staring at her. My stomach dropped. I crawled on the floor.

'What?' Tilly looked frozen, no expression at all, but I knew her mind was racing. Mine was too. Priests?

'What?' Sandra echoed, looking confused.

'Priests?' Tilly said.

'Yeah, last week?' Sandra said as if this was common knowledge. 'When they went over to Dudley, remember? They did the whole priest thing again.'

'Again?' My mum was like stone.

'For doing the cards, Tilly,' Sandra said.

My mum's face fell. Sandra realized she had untied the bag and the cat was about to scratch.

'Doing the cards?' Tilly sat up straight. 'Doing cards? Credit cards?'

'Yeah, Tilly, I thought you knew.' Sandra had red cheeks. 'That's why we're here in the first place – so they have new ground to do the cards.'

Sandra lit a cigarette and I saw her hand shaking. She was already in Keith's bad books.

I expected my mum to burst out crying, it was what she usually did when she was disappointed. I really thought she would but that's not what happened. She stood up, banging her thighs against the flimsy table so all the empty cans fell over, and she zipped her furry black hoodie right up to her chin and left the caravan. I tried to follow her, but I didn't see where she went.

Winning the talent show, all the fun we'd had, the smiles, the singing in the car, was worth nothing now. This was all a lie.

I walked around for a bit, trying to see where my mum had gone. Then I spotted her coming back from the direction of the holiday centre and so I followed her back to the van.

She sat at the table and resumed drinking.

'Now, see how he likes that,' she said.

'Tilly, what have you done?' Sandra said. She had picked the corner of the melamine table away. There was a metal patch showing through.

'Let's see how he likes that,' my mum said again, 'that lying bastard.'

Then my dad was back and Keith was back and the two couples were standing in between the caravans, with me sitting on the steps, and my mother was screaming first at my dad and then at Keith. 'You'll see what's what!'

Then Sandra was screaming at my mum.

'Shut up, you slag!' my mum screamed back at her.

And then everyone was shouting, and in the middle of it my dad was trying to pin down what exactly she had done to show him what was what, since that's all she kept repeating over and over.

Then the police came and everyone knew what Tilly had done. Drunk, hurt and angry, she had called them. When they took my dad and Keith away she was so so sorry for it, but it was too late.

It was as if she called them to bring on the pain. That's what I think anyway. She wanted it over and done with. No point waiting. He was going to get caught eventually and she was the one who suffered the most when he did, she was the one left to survive outside with all of us. It was easy in prison in comparison.

We were left in the caravan park with no way back home. My mum packed up the car and drove, even though she had no licence and didn't know how to drive. She drove that car with sheer courage and determination up the motorway to our house and burned the clutch out. I could see in her then a bravery that was inspiring as she cried and screamed with fear on that huge road, trucks and buses passing and other cars honking her for being in the wrong lane. She was terrified, but she was getting the job done.

Maybe I got my determination from my mum. And maybe I got my resilience from her. Maybe she and I are the same people, but she just met the wrong man.

The guilt she felt after Mablethorpe had her fall back into drinking and drugs, and while Dad was gone life went back to hell again. He ended up in custody in Lincolnshire for over a year.

8

When my dad got out of prison my parents were determined to stay clean, as usual. So I was on high alert, as
usual. My magical thinking was that I would in some
way be able to keep them on the straight and narrow if I
pried and spied into every aspect of their existence. I
checked through their pockets, looked through their
drawers and letters. I slid my hand between the cushions
of the couch when I sat beside them.

If I found something, a lighter or a packet, I'd take it
with me when I left the room. They couldn't ask for
something they swore they didn't use. I couldn't relax
and, to be honest, it was worse than when they were
using. When my parents were clean it was like sitting at
the top of a roller coaster, never knowing just when it
would tip, wobble and free-fall.

They'd try so hard, bullying each other, accusing each
other, a battle with each of them trying to control the
other's addiction, telling each other what they needed
or didn't need. Then they'd give in.

When they gave in, I would feel this huge

disappointment, a real grief for the promise of something I had only briefly glimpsed: a normal family life. Parents that cared. Clean clothes and good food. Like other kids had. It was like that for a little while after my dad came out of jail and moved us all to Birmingham.

Then John Bean came back up the road.

I saw him coming. And through the smiles and waves, I saw a monster. A demon. A man coming to lure my parents back into hell because he wanted company down there. The grim reaper.

I flew into the house before he got there, told my parents. 'John Bean is coming,' I said, and my brother Michael stood up from the table and walked out of the back door with a curse. We all knew. I fell asleep that night to a lullaby of reggae bass and loud voices.

The next morning when I went downstairs, John Bean was lying on our couch, asleep. A cigarette he had lit had made a scorch across the ashtray as it burned away untouched from top to end. I smushed the ash with my finger and looked on the floor for coins. And as I did, I noticed the carpet was pulled back from under the legs of the couch and a floorboard was loose. When I lifted it there was a bag, the 'works', the plastic already dripping with the brown and bloody needles of a junkie.

When we moved to Birmingham, I'd changed school and met my best friend, Louise. By the time we were thirteen we were playing at being grown up, smoking, chatting about things we knew nothing about and trying to avoid getting into cars with joyriders. We didn't mind keeping sketch, watching for the police or adults who might catch them, as the boys we hung around with broke into cars. They'd put on a show for us most times, spinning in front of the Poolway shopping centre, where we usually hung out. Sometimes they'd push us into getting in, and the way the car felt as it screeched around corners was terrifying.

In the youth club that pressure went away. None of the kids from the Poolway went there, just me and Louise, and so we could let go and be the little kids we actually were. We chased each other around, danced our heads off and laughed and laughed.

There were two youth workers there, a teacherly woman who kept us all in check with a wagging finger and eyes that never stopped rolling at you, and Mel.

Mel was around thirty, maybe forty, when I knew him. All the kids in the club loved Mel. He smoked a lot and kids like me would hover around him at the door, looking for a drag off the end. He always obliged. Trust is built in unethical ways with kids living in war zones. I trusted Mel and he became something of a mentor to me over the years.

'How's the mam and dad?' he would drop into conversation, after asking me to help him make tea or sort out a cupboard.

'Drinking,' I might say, or 'Drugging.' Depending.

'And how is Michael?' he would ask then. 'Still in the butcher's?'

I said yeah. My brother had left school early and he was working in a butcher's shop near where my baby sister went to nursery school. He dropped her in and collected her on his way to and from work.

'And how is the baby?'

'Getting big,' I said.

I trusted Mel fully, and so I told him everything. I told him about my mum prostituting, about Mablethorpe and my dad doing cards and my mum telling on him. I told him about my nanny dying and the funeral and that my dad wasn't allowed out for the day to go to it because it was my mum's mother, not his, and how much he cried when we went on a visit after the funeral. I told him that my dad was out now, and they were trying to stay off gear but that my dad was drinking all the time. I told him my mum was too. After Mablethorpe, my mum went downhill. Guilt, on top of everything else, was a catalyst for disaster. Our new house filled with cans and bottles and random boozers asleep on the couch. Once again our fridge remained empty and our toilet paper ran out and our towels piled up, wet and smelly, on the floor. The hope was gone from the house. She was drinking all the time and even when my dad got out of prison she didn't stop.

I told Mel all of that as if he didn't already know on sight who I was and what I was coming from. He never said much back, never had much of an opinion on any of it. He always just nodded along like I was telling him the weather. And no matter what I said, he was on my side. If I said my parents were bastards, then they were bastards. If I said they were angels, then that was what they were. He was the king of the safe space. A builder of confidence.

'You're a great person,' he said to me regularly. 'I think you'll go far. Yeah, school is a pain, but it's a means to an end – just get the GCSEs.'

I always moaned when he said things like that and told him that was ridiculous, but the words he said had an effect. They gave me some self-belief. Praise can be a fuel of survival in the education system for kids like me.

I'd take a heroin addict parent over an alcoholic one any day of the week. That may seem surprising but there is a meanness in booze and a horrible unpredictability that you just don't get with heroin addiction.

On heroin Tilly was a slow-moving void, a faint shadow of herself. She was gentle. She didn't shout, or call out, or embarrass me. She was dazed and manage-able. A quiet thing. When she drank she was unbearable.

The youth club was my place. I was free of everything there. So my chest grew instantly tight when I saw my mum coming through the door of the youth club. I saw the way other kids sniggered at her and looked at me. I knew what was happening when they'd take her hand and dance with her, turning her under their arm so she would lose her balance and fall over on the floor. She was laughing and thinking it was great; they were laughing too, thinking it was harmless to egg on the clown, *Go on, Tilly.* But that was my mother, so I wasn't laughing at all. It happened too often.

She would be fun and games at first and then suddenly turn. The laughing kids would back up then. Her face would change into the devil's, and she would hiss and spit what she really thought. The words came out like knives.

'You're something else, aren't you?' Cuts in my direction. I'd try to ignore it.

Here we go.

'Pretty as a picture, lovely . . . figure and all of it . . . they're mad about you, aren't they?'

Drunks have this way of speaking; the words boil up out of them having simmered for a while.

'You all think Katriona is gorgeous, don't you?' she asked the crowd. The kids stared.

Her words seemed generous, complimentary, but the way she said them, it was like a dog whistle. Only I could hear what she really meant. Only I knew she didn't think it too. And that hurt. That side of Tilly, you didn't get that with heroin.

*

Michael came home from his butcher's shop job once, with the youngest in his arms, and we were all absolutely starving. Tilly was up at the shopping centre drinking. She used to go there and hang out with all these old alcoholic boys, the kind of men who have been drinking so long they are missing fingers and have ulcers on their faces and legs. God knows where my dad was.

'Jesus Christ,' was all Michael said, and he handed the child to me and turned round and left the house again. At first we thought he was going to go back to work, but he walked in the other direction and headed down the road. 'He's definitely going to get Mum,' Matthew said.

He *was* going to get Mum. We saw him ten minutes later, striding across the green with Tilly over his shoulder. Her arms were swinging, weighed down by the exhaustion of alcohol in her system, but now and again she would wriggle and slap his shoulders and we could hear her say, 'Put me down, Michael,' but he didn't bother. Not until he got her all the way up the path and into the kitchen. He dropped her right on to her feet and she tried to sit down on the floor, but he yanked her back up and held her arms up until she stood.

'You,' he said, 'hey, mother of the year?'

Tilly's gaze wandered around until she found him.

'Yeah, you,' he said and pointed at the cooker, where Tilly had started something earlier and lost interest. She hadn't meant to starve us. She just got distracted. A pot with steeping potatoes never put on to boil. 'Cook for your kids,' he said.

She stared at him, helpless. 'Don't be like that. I can't help it, Michael.'

'Yes, you can, you're a grown woman and their mother,' he said. 'Act like it, please.' He handed her a knife and pulled a bag of frozen sausages out of the freezer and banged it on the counter.

When we were finally eating, I sat there looking from Mum to Michael to Mum again. I wondered what kind of family this was, where the kids were the parents. Michael was the one working out the money and keeping things ticking over when Tilly fell apart with addiction and my father was in prison. It was Michael who switched off lights to save the pennies and got me up for school and made us school lunches if we had bread. It was Michael who would tell you with his eyes to shut up and not start.

One of the worst things you could do to my parents was bring trouble to the door. And in my parents' eyes trouble was usually anything in the shape of an authority, or anyone who could call or would call an authority. To them the authorities would take your money, your house, your drugs or your kids.

So if we did anything that would bring that sort of trouble to the door it was massive. I remember being crouched up in the top corner of my bunk bed as my father roared at me, blue in the face. My judge and jury, full of alcohol, barring the door of my room at the top of the stairs in our house in Blakenhale Road.

I'd been caught mitching. Me and Louise had bunked school and hung around the shops for the day until my mother spotted me on her way back from the centre.

When my dad was in a rage he just went on and on. 'You're grounded,' he said, and then banged the heel of his hand on the bed frame.

'I'm going out!' I said. There was no way I was missing the youth club. Me and Louise were in the school play, called *Dianella* – which was about Princess Diana – and we were practising every chance we got. It was why we had bunked off in the first place. Because we needed to learn the routines properly.

I'd never been given a part in a play before, and I was so excited. I was only new in the school, in the last year of primary, and the other girls didn't think I should have got it. So I had to do a good job.

'You are not going anywhere,' my dad said. His eyes looked glassy but that was the only indicator that Tony was drunk. He never lost his footing or slurred his words. His pupils got really small and he got meaner. 'You'll have that wag man here,' he said, talking about the truancy officer.

I was raging. Why did I even come home at all? I'd only done it because Louise's brother was annoying me, telling me that my mum and dad were looking for me. He was joking but it turned out they *were* looking for me. Now my dad was saying I couldn't go back out. It was a disaster.

'I'm going out!' I was going if he liked it or not.

'You're not going anywhere, you little SLUT!' He roared the word and it hung in the air between us like a firework. Then there was a bang, and another one. Then the heavy thuds of an angry man coming up the stairs.

My brother Michael.

'See you?' He grabbed my dad by the collar and pushed him back into the wall of my room. Michael's nose was pressed into my dad's forehead. He stood over him.

My dad went limp; it was strange to see that. He looked sideways. Submission. Michael was a tower over him, a solid tower. The kind that keeps you safe.

'Don't! You! Ever! Speak like that! To her! Again!' Michael said, and he thumped my dad against the wall with every word.

I took the opportunity to squeeze past them and out of the room, down the stairs and out of the door. I ran down the road, relieved.

When Michael made us learn off stories about what rides we went on so we could pretend to Nanny that we'd had the best day ever on the money she gave us to go to the fair with, money we had lost on the way, Michael showed me who he was.

When he slept pressed into the wall, knees bent, so our dog, Bonzo, could have the full stretch of the bed, or when he would wrap us in a blanket and throw us down the stairs to hear us squeal with delight because our mother was out making our lives a misery, he showed me who he was.

When he had his heart broken, listening to 'their' song on repeat to keep the feelings lingering as long as he could, not wanting to move on or let go, he showed me who he was.

Michael was always someone I could trust. He showed me that all the time, in everything he did. Even when he was telling me things I didn't want to hear, he always made me understand that, as far as he was concerned, I mattered. He was in my corner. I didn't have many people like that over the years, but I always knew I had Michael. Michael was mum, dad and brother all in one. I saw him as the problem solver. I depended on him so much. I still do.

And now when he sends me songs, just a link to YouTube with no message, it's always something from back then, a reference or memory. Something we loved, something to offer me as evidence that we both went through all of that and we are both still here. That's who my brother has always been. Someone who knows me well. One of four others who witnessed my childhood.

Being a sibling in a family like ours is hard. We have had our spats and real fallings-out, but we love each other, even when it gets so complicated and so deep that we can't talk to one another. At the end of the day, we have our shared history and though the way we remember may be different, we have the common bond of our mad childhood. Even if we can't talk it through face to face, we always have that keeping us tied.

Blanchardstown,
3 June 2022

Hi Matt,

It's me, your sister Katriona. I wanted to write to you because I've been talking about you a lot lately, with this book. Remembering all the shit that went on in our house hasn't been easy, but one thing it's reminded me of is how much I love you. I suppose I want you to know that. I miss you and I love you and that's why I'm writing to you.

Them little kids we were, the ones who got up early and made sugar sandwiches, leaving sugar all over the counter, the kids who left hours before school so we could get there first and have the playground to ourselves, them little kids are still in us somewhere, even though we changed, even though things happened, and we did things. It's still us.

I was laughing this morning talking about that time we arrived at school, looked at each other, and turned straight back around. We communicated without words, didn't we? You and me were connected like that.

So, we walked into Coventry where the market was — you know, the big one that used to be on, don't think it is now, it sold fish and crap and people were all shouting different things at the one time. And we went around helping ourselves to the stalls, two little thieves with bright eyes and smiles. Brats.

We took those paints, remember? You had red and yellow, I think, and I had green and blue, tiny jars of watery paint from a stall that we used to flick patterns on the passing coats as people walked by.

We went to Pool Meadow then, didn't we? Down where the buses are all parked up overnight and we pulled the doors open and got on board looking for the trays of coins that buses had. You sat in the driver's seat and said, 'Let's take the bus,' which made me laugh because you always had to go that step further, you always pushed the boat out to make me laugh.

And things changed after Bob hurt me, because he picked me to do that to and not you. Maybe I just found it too hard to be around anyone, I didn't know who I was any more, so I broke our connection and we never got it back. In many ways my life story is the story of losing you. A story told through stories that you have too.

Even though Mum was softer with you and Dad was softer with me, it never mattered to us, because we just wanted each other.

I remember being so excited that you were finally coming to school with me, but you didn't want to go. You kicked our mum on the steps because you wanted to stay with her, and I was angry with you for that. You were darkening the door of the place I loved, at least I did then, because I was in Mrs Arkinson's class, and she loved me and made me feel as if I was worth something. And in some ways, you did that all along, both in good ways and bad.

From watching you scream your head off the first day of school, to knowing where you are now, has been a path of hurt and turmoil for both of us. No matter what, you are my brother. We were in the trenches together, you and me. Weren't we? Down there we knew each other so well. Even in the dark.

But I climbed out. I thought if I climbed out, I could pull you all out too, with me, to stand on solid ground. I wanted you to see the light and feel the freedom.

And I think about that, standing on the top of the trench, and you're still down there. Because I cut the rope. I was trying to pull everyone up, but the weight of it was dragging me back down so I cut the rope. And you were one of the ones that fell. I couldn't save you. I couldn't save Mum or Dad, or anyone. I could only save myself. And it's something I wish was different but it's how it is.

You've done such terrible things, but I still see you for who you are, the kid brother who made everything easier. The kid who suffered like I did, although in different ways. The one who pushed the boat out so I would lose myself in laughter and forget the pain.

You're my brother, Matthew, and only the five of us remember what it was like when we were small.

Katriona x

9

When I think about being a teenager, the first bit is always me and Louise. We spent most of our time in fits of laughter, in class and out. We clicked. I never fought much with her, but when we did, the energy we put into making each other laugh instead went into killing each other.

'I'm keeping it, it's mine,' she said to me on the hill down from our house, aged eleven, where we had just been trick-or-treating. There were three of us, me, Louise and my other best friend, Julie. We had split up to go house to house with an agreement that any money we got would be shared out, but Louise had been given a pound and now the contract was frustrated.

'You are not!' I said.

'Yes, I am,' she said.

Then I said she was a money-grabbing bitch, just like her mother.

To this day I don't know why I said it, a slur I'd heard about others which seemed suitable to drive my point home. The minute her mouth dropped open I knew I was in for it, and I was right. She pulled her arm up and back and thumped me right in my face. And then she did it again.

So I thumped her back. She grabbed me around the neck, and we fell over. Thumping, pulling hair and screaming. We rolled about on the ground, hitting and beating each other in fits of temper, and I remember the reason I fought so hard was because I was sure this was it, she would never be my friend again, and so I wanted to hurt her for all the pain that this would cause me.

She was my friend, my source of laughter and light, and I was sure I didn't have her any more. But I needn't have fought so hard, she never left me.

Her aunt ran a charity shop in town and on Saturdays we would meet there, going through the stock for the best bits and finding amusement in the donations.

'Woo-hoo!' Louise held up a wedding dress out of a white zipped bag. Before I knew it, she was slipping into the corset. 'Do me up, Kat,' she said, and I did.

'There's another one, look,' she said, pulling a veil out of a plastic wrapper and pressing it into her hair. She pointed at another white dress bag with the words *Ken's Bridal Shop* printed across the front.

I pulled the dress out as fast as I could, stepping in and dragging it up my body over my shoulders and turning so my friend could zip me up. We stared at each other, two brides, and then exploded into laughter.

'Come here,' I said, grabbing her arm and pulling her

to the front of the shop and into the window. I pushed things out of the way and fixed my veil.

I stood still, one arm up and one arm down.

She did too. Desperately holding my laughs behind my teeth, I squeaked. She snuffed giggles through her nose. We were two mannequins in a shop window.

An old lady and her son crossed the road. And as they did, as soon as the man's eyes lifted from the road to the path ahead, I jumped up and let out a scream like a banshee.

'Jesus CHRIST!' He stumbled with the fright. The old woman clutched her chest.

Louise opened her mouth and screamed too. And it turned into a laugh, and it was so funny I fell forward, clutching at my friend in absolute glee. We laughed ourselves sick, tumbling out of the window in our dresses on to the shop floor and recounting the story again and again.

'You nearly gave the ol' dear a heart attack!' Louise said, and it was the funniest thing I could think of.

'I swear he pissed his self,' I said.

'Let's look in the bags,' Louise said, calming herself, 'need new leggings.'

She had leggings of every colour and print, that one. First dibs from the charity shop. It was good for me because I had nothing and so I borrowed her clothes. She would come over to my house and sit in the kitchen chatting to my mum and dad while I changed into whatever leggings she brought me to wear that night. She always sat there as if everything was normal. Ignored the mounting ashtrays and the bottles.

We would put on shows for my parents, dances and bits from *French & Saunders*, entertaining them with our enthusiasm as they sat on the couch, stoned or drunk, laughing at every move we made. Small pockets of sunshine in the storm.

Louise always looked past my parents' troubles; they were my parents so she loved them by proxy, through me. For me. She loved my whole family, always around, always in and out.

So many of my milestone stories from my childhood have Louise in them. When I got my first period she was there, sitting in the passenger seat of my brother Michael's van with red cheeks, embarrassed as he had given her the news himself. My mother had told him as he left the house to give us girls a lift to town.

When I realized why she was mortified, I rolled my eyes and scolded Michael for telling my business.

'She needs to know,' he said, letting off the handbrake with authority.

Me and Louise, we had a friendship that worked really well. And still works. Apart from our boxing match on the hill that Halloween, we never really fell out. And even when we did have small tiffs, it wasn't for long. Louise is the kind to leave you be and come back later.

Nobody was funnier than us two together, nobody could match it. We always came back to each other.

In our later teens we'd go out down the Macka-down, an area named for the pub in the centre of it, just to cause trouble; and we would go there with the boys to fight the Glebe gang, named for the other big local pub. I fought with boys too. We stole cars and flew them around corners, every one of us pretending we didn't care about any of it, but feeling terrified inside, leaving the cars burning on corners as if they were litter. That twenty-minute joyride, that roller coaster of excitement – would we crash? would we hit something? would we get chased by the police? – it was happiness. This sounds crazy, but it was mood modification, the same reason people do drugs – chasing a buzz.

I was arrested three times as a kid, for fighting, rob-bing and drugs. Hanging around with the kind of kids I did got you into trouble. We would be robbing sheds and selling drugs, egging each other on. I went to pubs and hung out with much older kids and went to places that, when I look back, I wish I hadn't. Kids don't see danger the way adults do.

We took our pain out on the people we thought deserved it – the people who had it all. You're not born with a chip on your shoulder, but it's hewn in as you grow. When it seems like, no matter what you do, you're pushed down anyway. And if you're not pushed down, you're pulled down by your own – accused of getting ideas about yourself, thinking you're better than them. You can't win. So you just give in to it.

But with Louise, when it was just the two of us, we would laugh and dance, talking about boys and romance and what we wanted in life, saying anything that came into our heads and never worrying about how it would come across. We were as free as we could be for the time we had together, before the others came along and we would have to revert to cool.

My school had a uniform. I was glad of it, like I had been in Brownies. I appreciated the opportunity to blend in. From a distance, at least, to be part of a colony of ants, one of many.

Close up, I was still the poor kid. Like I'd always been.

I was never popular in school, I was never that kid in the middle of a bunch, holding court from class to class. I was the other one, the one shuffling through with old socks and holes in my cuffs that I picked at and no smile. I was the kid with her face hidden under her hair as she made her way to class. I wanted to be ignored.

School was a conflict, a constant one. I wanted the information that you got in the classroom, but I found the authority factor difficult. The way school is set up, it doesn't suit all kids and it didn't suit me. I hated the interactions, the questions, the conversations, the day-to-day administration of being a pupil in a modern-day school.

It's hard to describe that conflict. The tug between wanting the education but not wanting to have to deal with everything that goes along with it. I think shame has so much to do with the decisions I made during school. I didn't want to be seen. My family and what we were, what we did, I knew we were frowned upon and looked down on. I was stressed and angry all the time, so any comment or question in my direction was met with aggression.

I was lonely and totally frustrated. I wanted another life, not this one. I hated being around people who had what I wanted: nice homes, good clothes and food, love. I believed they had those things because they were better than me. They had done something right and I had done something wrong. I really wanted those things, but I didn't know how to get them, I didn't even know I could strive for things at all.

I didn't like how I felt around the kids in school who did well. I didn't trust any of them. Even if they showed an interest in me, they'd soon find out who I was and turn their backs. I kept my distance.

Nobody ever showed me a future or how to change things for myself. Nobody ever asked me what I wanted or set out steps to achieve it. My report cards were always the same.

Has potential. Must focus more. Attendance needs improving.

They might as well have said anything at all, my parents never looked at them. They never went to parent–teacher evenings because they didn't – or couldn't – care how we did at school. They didn't care if we went or not, they just didn't want us to bring authority to our house.

I remember answering the door one night and my English teacher Mr Pickering was standing there, looking smaller and younger than he ever did in school. He asked to speak to my dad. My stomach dropped. A teacher at the door. My dad was in the sitting room, drunk. But I called him anyway and stood back behind the door.

Mr Pickering was a northern man in his forties. I loved him. I loved his pronunciation of Shakespeare, the way he thoughtfully read through the texts and explained each phrase to us, telling us how we might say it today. I took notes in his class, always wanting to make good on my homework. His praise meant more to me than other teachers'.

I wanted to be the best in his class; he was hard on all of us, so you knew when he told you that you'd done well, you really had. In his class I gladly shot my hand up; even wrong answers were engaged with. We read Shakespeare, *The Merchant of Venice*, following Antonio as he is pursued for money by Shylock, the Jewish lender.

'Who is the victim here?' Mr Pickering said, looking up at us, panning his eyes around.

There was a flurry of hands up. One by one, wrong answers thoughtfully processed.

Then me.

'Shylock, sir,' I said. Some of the girls laughed.

He half smiled, stood up from his desk and walked around it, leaning against the lip of the desk and folding his arms.

'Shylock?' he said.

I nodded. I was sure of this. 'He's always being pushed and called names because he's a Jew, sir,' I said. 'Nobody is being nice to him . . . and he lent the money, Antonio is in the wrong to not give it back.'

'Spot on, Katriona,' he said. 'Lots of insight!'

I had 'gotten it' – the point – and it felt so good. I wondered if I could come up with more things like that.

Teachers like Mr Pickering foster that feeling in kids, and they are brilliant at it. Kids like me thrive on 'getting it' and want more of that feeling. Approval kept me coming back to school.

He never mollycoddled any of us, least of all me.

'You could take a leaf out of Louise's book, Katriona,' he said one day, looking from my written work to hers. It was flippant. But it hurt.

'She didn't even do it, sir,' I said, dropping Louise in it, but my blood was boiling. Louise hadn't done her homework, her mother had. I worked so hard on mine, but I could never be as neat and tidy as a forty-year-old woman with nothing better to do. 'Her mother did it for her, sir.'

Louise turned in her seat and I stared back at her. I flashed my eyebrows. Her jaw dropped and she whispered 'Stop it' at me in disgust.

Mr Pickering didn't flinch, but he did frown, at *me*. And he pressed his lips into a thin line. He disapproved of my disloyalty, but I didn't care. He sat back at his desk and started marking something.

Louise glared and whispered, 'What did you tell on me for?'

I shrugged. 'Do your own homework,' I whispered back.

I would have thrown anyone under the bus for praise from that man. But I learned that day that deflection won't work as deception. Regardless of who did Louise's homework, it was better than mine.

At the end of lunch that day, Mr Pickering called me up. 'If you're not busy now perhaps you'd give me a hand?'

I would. I was delighted at the opportunity to redeem myself. We walked down to the office together and he showed me what to do. Then he set about making two cups of tea.

As I stood there beside the copier while hot sheets of text were spat out, one on top of the other, Mr Pickering handed me half of his sandwich as if it was the most normal thing in the world.

'Do you read?' he asked me. 'For fun, I mean.'

I nodded. I ate the sandwich in gulps, and it was hard to breathe because I was eating so fast.

He raised his eyebrows, handed me the other half. 'What do you read?'

I shrugged; I couldn't come up with a list. I read everything, anything I could find.

'Have you a favourite book?' he asked, making it easier.

I couldn't answer. Not really. I just read whatever my dad read.

'How do you like *The Merchant of Venice*?' he asked. I didn't know what to say.

'You have good insight into the characters and story,' he said. 'I noticed that in class.'

I shrugged again but I liked the sound of that.

Mr Pickering told me he was from the north, where the mines were.

'I've never seen a mine,' I said, 'but I read a book once . . . they were mining in it and it collapsed . . . or something like that.'

'Sounds like an interesting book,' he said.

'Just one of my dad's,' I said. 'He reads all the time, so I just read the books after him, when he's finished.'

'What else have you read?'

'Oh, honestly, whatever,' I said. 'I just read whatever. My dad likes scary books, like horror, so I read those too.'

Mr Pickering looked amused. He tilted his head.

'My dad reads whatever books my mum can get down the charity shop,' I explained, 'all sorts of rubbish, but sometimes you get a good one.'

'I was a miner, you know, myself,' he said.

I looked at him. Tried to visualize him covered in black dust. I couldn't imagine that as he stood there in his clean beige jumper and grey slacks. His shirt was crisp white.

'I worked in mines from when I was thirteen,' he said. His accent was long and nasal. 'We didn't think there was anything else but to work in the mines.'

'So how come you became a teacher?' I said.

'I'll tell you – I was down those mines day in day out, listening to the other men talking about this and that, and all I could think about was me books at home,' he said. 'And every day when I came home I was happier to see those books than me mam or dad or anyone.'

I understood that.

'We worked very hard down there,' he said, 'no light and barely enough to survive being paid to you at the end of the week, and one day –' he sighed and unfolded his arms, put his cup of tea down – 'I thought I just needed something better than all of it.'

'Did you quit?' I felt so surprised. I knew this man as Mr Pickering, Mr P, the English teacher. In my head he was born an English teacher. I couldn't imagine him down a mine, breaking his back.

'I started to study at night,' he said, 'swapped the novels for schoolbooks and just kept going until I had my degree.'

I nodded. 'Did you want to be a teacher, Mr Pickering?'

'I didn't know what I wanted,' he said. 'I just wanted something else but that mine.' He clapped his hands. 'Now,' he said, 'let's get these papers sorted.'

We worked in silence for a while.

'I might have some novels lying around that you can have,' Mr Pickering said. 'Have you read *Of Mice and Men*?'

I shook my head.

'I'll bring some books in tomorrow for you,' he said, 'and you can tell me what you think.'

I really wanted the books. He brought them as promised. Small paperbacks in different colours. I read them at night in my bunk.

'So what did you think?' he asked me a few weeks later when I told him I'd finished them.

Somehow, through talking to him about *Of Mice and Men* and *Emma* and all of those amazing books in the weeks and months that followed, as the lunchtime copier errand became a weekly routine, through the books we discussed, I talked about my life. I wasn't really aware of it, but as we discussed the characters in the books we discussed me and found solutions and ways through my own problems.

Mr Pickering never really said much, in the way of advice to me at least, he usually just nodded along and his chin would pucker in the harder parts. Like when I would get hypothetical and talk about how a kid might manage if their parents were bad with drink.

When he came to the door I was worried I had done something wrong. I stood behind the door and listened as Mr Pickering spoke to my dad.

'I was hoping to see you this evening at the parents' night, Mr O'Sullivan,' he said, 'but you didn't come.'

My dad mumbled something in the way of an excuse, leaning against the doorway.

'Katriona is an excellent student, gifted, and has great potential to continue with school and college. She needs support from home and you aren't giving her that.' He stalled for a moment. 'You should be ashamed of yourselves.'

My dad became apologetic, sounding like a child when he spoke. He wanted the door shut and the issue over. 'We'll come next time,' he said, 'we will do better by her, thanksmisterpickering.'

It was the first time I ever saw my dad like that.

He shut the door.

'Sorry, love,' he said and shuffled back to the couch. I heard a can crack.

I didn't care. What my dad thought didn't matter, I was thrilled at what Mr Pickering had said to him. I was an excellent student.

10

The first time I had sex was in an old garage down the road from my house. The boys I hung around with smoked weed there sometimes. We were delinquents after all, often breaking into sheds to steal stuff we could sell. We found one of them abandoned.

Me and this boy went there, just the once. For a whole year, every single night, while he'd spun cars and messed with his friends, I'd waited on the sidelines until he was ready to walk me home. I knew he liked me, I could feel it when we were alone. He was affectionate and sweet to me then. But around his friends he ignored me. And after a year when he made it clear that *I* was making it hard for him to control himself, that we might have to break up, I felt guilty. So I had sex with him.

And now, walking home afterwards, he was grinning from ear to ear. He kept kissing me and he was holding my hand. He would be good to me now.

'You're some girl, Kat,' he said and pulled me under his arm with a squeeze. I was so happy. I knew I'd done the right thing. I needn't have worried. We were going to stay together now for sure.

'Shit, is that your dad?' He suddenly pushed me away from him and I looked up to see my dad and our dogs standing at the top of the hill. He'd spotted me.

'You!' he roared. 'Get in!'

'I'm coming for God's sake, Dad,' I shouted back. He roared again. A light went on in the house across the way.

'Go on, then,' the boy said and turned on his heel.

I caught up to my dad, who was standing there looking furious.

I wondered, could he tell? Only ten minutes earlier I'd been having sex, standing up in the back of a shitty shed. I decided no. If he knew he would kill me. My dad was a mess in himself, but he had high hopes for us.

When we got back to our house, I ran up the stairs and climbed into the top bunk and lay there. The baby was awake in the bottom bunk. She called my name and I hung over the side and looked at her.

'Go to sleep,' I said.

Her eyes were bright in the dark. 'Go to sleep,' I said again.

She shook her head.

'If you don't go to sleep, I'll run away to London,' I said.

She shut her eyes tight.

I lay there in the dark thinking about the sex I'd just had. It hadn't felt scary like the abuse had years ago. It just felt a bit boring and weird. But the smile on the boy's face had felt amazing. The way he hugged and kissed me after. I wanted that.

My first real crush was a boy called Luke Healy. I was twelve. Louise totally indulged me on it. She was great that way. She would talk to me for hours, building all sorts of future scenarios for the two of us with the boys we liked. When we were doing the play, *Dianella*, the two leads had been boys we fancied, and we had done the same. But this was different. This time I wanted to tell Luke.

'Don't do it.' Louise slid down the wall. 'I'll die if you do, I'll actually die, Kat.'

'I'll miss you,' I said and stuck my tongue out. I was determined. I was going to tell Luke Healy that I fancied him and that was that. I was going to ask him out.

Luke was in my year. And over the summer he had stretched up into the coolest boy I knew. He wore his trousers tight and his tie short. He looked like the singers on the TV. And I was sure, by now, that he liked me back. He looked at me all the time, and when I looked back, he blushed. He always had something to tell me in the mornings, and he always left the class when I did and walked along with me.

'Wait for him to ask you, Kat,' Louise warned, 'you'll make a bloody fool of yourself. Girls don't ask boys out!'

I didn't see why that was the unwritten rule. I had a sense of unfairness at twelve; I didn't want to be submissive and wait around in the hope that a boy would ask me out. It seemed stupid and I was going against the grain.

'Don't do it, Kat,' she pleaded, 'I'll just die.'

'Die then,' I said and snapped my chewing gum.

Luke wasn't the only one who had transformed over the summer. I had too. My body had got curves. I felt desire and I didn't want to wait to feel the reward of it. I wanted to kiss and hold hands. It seemed that maybe I could find something warm here; the way Luke Healy looked at me, it felt like someone could really care about me.

'Just because I'm a girl, I have to pretend I don't care?' I was not convinced. 'Sounds like rubbish to me.'

Louise shook her head.

'Go ask him to talk to me,' I said. She shook it again. I insisted.

So, rolling her eyes, she stood up and went off in the direction of Luke, who was standing with a bunch of lads by the wall. Luke looked over at me and I smiled at him. He looked away with red cheeks.

Louise gave him the message and returned with him, walking slightly behind her. The boys he was with made fools of themselves, whooping and hitting each other.

'Come for a walk?' I said, fixing my ponytail with the nonchalance of a woman who knew what she was doing. We walked along and at the end of the path I turned and said, 'Will you go out with me?' And he said 'Yeah' with the biggest smile and so I kissed his cheek and felt a surge of power in my heart. I was my own woman.

For a brief moment in 1988, before the patriarchy knocked me back into line, I felt like I could make it. For those few weeks, before we fizzled out and stopped holding hands, I had everything I wanted. I wouldn't feel like that again for a long time. Within a year or two that empowered feisty girl had been worn down. My body, which kept developing more curves, invited wolf whistles and gropes from old men on the train. I hated it.

My whole life I'd watched my dad and his friends size up women in the pages of newspapers. All men took part in that, it was normal. My dad encouraged my brothers too. Some models passed the test. *A cracker. Great tits. Good arse.* Some didn't.

But when men started appraising me, I was frightened. They slowed down their cars and shouted from the window, they whispered in my ear as they passed, they groped me. I was nothing more than an object to them. It was a free-for-all.

This body I had, the one that I lived in, was working against me. There was nothing I could do about the shape of it. I couldn't change it. And there was nothing I could do about how men were looking at it. But I was blamed for that anyway.

'*I see you're getting your boobs*' – said to me as I stood in my Brownie uniform, aged nine, by my dad's friend Jerry as he sat smoking on our couch.

'*Great tits, lovely*' – said to me, aged thirteen, by a man on the bus as he stood beside me waiting to get off at his stop. He stared down my school shirt.

'*Them's blow-job lips*' – said to me by the dad of one of the other girls as I stood at the school gates with my friend, aged fourteen. The man had stains all down his front from his breakfast.

Sometimes I wonder what would happen if middle-aged women spoke to boys the way middle-aged men speak to girls. Imagine a twelve-year-old boy standing at the school gates and the mother of one of his friends approaching him and saying something about how well he was filling out his trousers. It would be, rightly, considered a shocking and hugely disturbing thing to say.

At twelve, at thirteen, at fourteen, I felt fully responsible for how men spoke to me and the way they groped me. I felt it was my fault when my teacher, Mr Higgins, stood so close I'd want to run. Or when Danny Roberts, down the back of the shopping centre, showed me his erection and said, 'Look what you've done.' It wasn't a con, he fully believed that was how it was – it was something I had *done* to him. 'You'll have to sort that for me now,' he said. I was terrified when he forced my hand down and tried to make me masturbate him.

I didn't know how I was responsible for any of this because what could I do to prevent it? I was wearing tracksuits just like the boys but I couldn't make my bum smaller, I couldn't hide my breasts. I started covering my mouth when I smiled, to stop my lips flattening out as they did against my teeth. I pressed them into a tight line when I smiled.

As a teenager with no love at home, and with male approval being the only gauge I had as to whether or not I was worth anything, I slipped from being a confident, ballsy feminist-minded kid to a girl who loitered outside the local shopping centre in case a boy I liked would want to see me before he went home. Sometimes he did, stopping on his way and taking me home with a kiss at the end of it. Sometimes he walked right by me.

In the movies, me and Louise watched bad boys being tamed by the love of a good woman. Love songs were about women 'standing by' bad men. I got the message. Too late, I understood that the movies and songs were a fantasy – in them the bad boy wasn't really bad after all. All he needed was love and once he had that he had it all. In the real world the bad boys don't care and they'll never care. Mine was no different.

And after all of it, all the years of being pushed down

and shoved back, when the boy I liked and wanted to be with got more distant, I tried harder, waited longer. So when he told me he might dump me because *'I'm just finding it hard to stop myself, Kat. I can't do this any more,'* I knew what the solution was. I wouldn't ask him to stop. That would be the making of me and him. We would be a real couple, then.

I was fifteen. Of course, I got pregnant.

There are two kinds of looks you get as a teen mother. Concern is one. Scorn is the other. In the UK and Ireland its mostly the latter and not enough of the former. When my friend Cynthia and I, aged fifteen, stood outside the British Pregnancy Advisory Service waiting to go in, the looks we got from passers-by were contemptuous.

I was there as a friend only. Or so I thought. Cynthia had been pregnant a few weeks ago and had taken the abortion pill. Now she was in a bit of a pickle.

'Ben doesn't know I did that,' she had told me that morning as we walked to school.

'He thinks you're still pregnant?' I said. 'Oh my God, Cynthia.' It was funny to me. 'What are you going to do?'

'Don't laugh!' Cynthia said, and we both saw Ben get off the bus. She waved and said hurriedly, 'I told him I was bleeding and having a miscarriage last night. He wants me to go to the bloody clinic now – you'll come with me, won't you?'

I had to, I supposed. Ben and Cynthia weren't easy to be around, they believed in public displays of passion. But I really didn't want to be in school that day and staying off alone was boring. I sighed and said okay.

'They won't let you in unless you're getting something done, Kat,' Cynthia told me, 'so get a test done or something so I won't be waiting on me own.'

I shrugged. 'Okay.'

Ben was waiting for us at the bus stop and as we crossed the road the bus came along. He put a protective arm around his girlfriend and kissed her ear. 'You all right, love?' he said. She looked as sad as she could. I rolled my eyes.

We got on the bus, straight up the stairs and down to the back where I took up two seats, sideways with my feet up. Cynthia and Ben sat together, entangled legs and arms.

'I hate this shit bus,' I said for the sake of it. They didn't answer, they were too busy kissing. I turned back, put my feet on the floor and looked out of the window.

The bus was on its way to the city centre. We were heading to Navigation Street, by the station, where the British Pregnancy Advisory Service offered free testing to anyone who needed it. I held the door for Cynthia as she told Ben to be brave and he told her to be strong. The minute we got in there and the door swung closed she grabbed my arm and whispered, 'I feel terrible, but

I don't want to upset him. He might break it off – I can't lose him.'

These were teenage dilemmas.

I signed in with her, ticking the box for pregnancy test. It was the easiest one. The other options were too invasive. Then me and Cynthia sat in the waiting room for what seemed like ages but was probably only fifteen minutes. The nurse came out and gave us both bottles and we went to the tiny bathroom off the hall and made a huge fuss over getting a wee into them. By the time we had it done we were in hysterics. There was no real anxiety here, it was just a ruse.

The nurse called me in. That first look, the one of concern, was all over her face.

'So, Katriona, your test is positive,' she said. She sat down and pulled her chair right up to mine so our knees touched. She had a clipboard on her knee.

'Thought so,' I said. 'That's good then, thanks.' I pulled my coat from the back of the chair on to my lap. I was going to go now.

'Good?' She leaned in. 'Katriona, you understand? The test is positive.'

'Yes!' I nodded so she knew I understood. 'It's positive.' Positive was the outcome I wanted. I believed that meant I was not pregnant. Pregnancy was a bad thing, negative was bad. Right?

'Katriona, you're pregnant,' she said.

I stared at her. The words were Greek, I didn't get it.

'You're pregnant,' she said again.

A slow dawning of what this meant spread across my chest and neck in a hot flush of understanding and absolute terror.

No.

'I couldn't be,' I said. I'd only done it once.

'You are pregnant, Katriona.' She touched my hand and I flicked it away.

Don't touch me.

'No,' I said, 'I'm not even supposed to be here. I only came in with Cynthia because she told her boyfriend she was pregnant when she'd already had an abortion.' I was baffled. What was this nightmare?

The nurse pressed three leaflets into my hand and I dropped them to the floor. I stood up so violently I fell back against the wall.

'No,' I said, 'no way.'

And I left.

I met Cynthia in the corridor coming out. She started fake crying the minute we neared the exit and kept it up for the whole journey on the yellow 96 bus back to the Poolway shopping centre. All the way back Cynthia and Ben consoled one another over their non-existent miscarriage and I sat there with the world falling apart and my heart broken.

The three of us got off the bus that evening at the

Poolway. Cynthia and Ben headed off to find a wall to sit on and cry. I stood at the bus stop as the bus drove away. I felt like I was made of glass. I knew I would never go back to school again. I couldn't face any of them, the kids, the boys. I couldn't let Mr Pickering down like this. It was all over.

I thought about the baby and I thought about myself and I never considered any other option. This was my destiny, and there was no changing it. It sounds strange considering where I had just come from and the services they would have provided me with free of charge. The truth is, being a young mother was my path and I knew it straight away. It doesn't mean I wasn't frightened and horrified.

I knew I was having the baby and so I went to the phone box across the street and called the boy.

'I'm pregnant,' I said. My entire body was shaking. The walls of the telephone were caving in.

There was a long pause.

'Look, Kat, I'm really tired,' he said, and he hung up.

11

I told my mum the minute I saw her. I walked into the house and she was standing at the kitchen door and I just told her. I couldn't hold on to that secret for a second. She stared at me for a minute, made me repeat it.

'I'm pregnant,' I said.

Her expression went from a blank stare to raised eyebrows and a smile. She clapped her hands, came for me and squeezed my arms, patting and rubbing them. Then she hugged me. I was confused, but relieved.

'This will be the making of you, Kat,' she said. 'This is what you need, this will settle you down and make things better.'

I didn't want to settle down. I thought about the shopping centre and the fun we had down there. The week before the boy had set a bin on fire round the back of the shops and we had all stood and watched it burn. He had slipped his arms around my waist, picked me up and swung me round in front of everyone.

'Don't tell Dad, Mum,' I begged. I held her arm.

'I won't, I won't,' she said. 'Go on up to bed now, get an early night.'

It wasn't even dinner time, but I was so exhausted and worn out I went anyway. I lay there in the bed wishing I had never gone to that shed. I wished I could rewind time and never so much as talk to any boy ever.

Then it was the morning and I had slept for twelve hours. I got up and went downstairs, passing my father's room where he was half sitting up in bed. His arms were folded and he stared at me. She'd told him even though I asked her not to. My stomach sank.

'So,' he said. He looked at me as if he was bored. It was a look I'd seen on his face before, his version of contempt.

'Dad, I'm sorry,' I said.

He reclined there on his stinking, filthy bed with his greasy hair and dirty teeth, and said, 'Congratulations in order? You're pregnant?'

I nodded. 'Yes, Dad,' I said. I wrapped my arms around myself and rubbed them.

He sat up straight suddenly, leaned towards me. He spoke with a tone of authority and said, 'Katriona, you do realize the odds are that you will have a child with a deformity or disability?' He coughed and repeated it again. 'The odds are very high of that.'

What?

A lump formed in my throat instantly and I was dizzy. Why was he saying something like that? I couldn't speak.

'You need to think about that, if you're planning . . .' He trailed off but waved his fingers in the direction of my stomach. His fingertips were yellow. The pillow he rested back against was yellow too from years of piss and drool.

'Why are you saying that?' I finally got the words out.

There was a malevolence to my dad when he was angry. He said, 'It's something you need to consider. We have five healthy kids – odds are you won't.'

I stood there staring. I knew that was rubbish. He waved his hand at me; I was being dismissed. I walked down the hall to the bathroom and cried my eyes out. I knew he wanted me to have an abortion, but he couldn't say that, not straight.

I left the house for school that day, but I didn't go. I sat down on the wall by the centre in a daze. Buses passed me full of people, friends from school banged on the window and mouthed my name. A van passed and the man in it whistled and when I looked up at him he licked his lips. A woman with a buggy crossed the road and I watched her till she went round the corner.

What is going to happen to me?

Then I stood up, leaving my useless school bag on the ground, and walked towards the shopping centre. I didn't even look back at the bag. That part of my life was over and I knew it. I couldn't see Mr Pickering. He thought I would go far, he had said so. But I was going to stay right here. No more classes, no more education. I was done. I had ruined my life. I dropped out of school unofficially, never said anything, and nobody from the school ever came to our house. One of the kids must have told them I was pregnant and they just signed off on me then and there.

I spent the next few months walking around the centre or lying in bed or on the couch. The boy wasn't saying much. I was lectured by his mother. She saw me as a siren, luring and trapping her innocent son into this situation. I spent the time apologizing for what I had done to him. I felt guilty and regretful for getting myself into this situation.

I remember seeing a newspaper headline which informed the public of an 'epidemic' of young teenage girls deliberately becoming pregnant in order to sponge off the taxpayer. It explained the harsh faces and tuts from strangers.

Then one night I came in and my whole family were around the table. It looked like some church meeting but with drink and cigarettes. My brothers had red eyes; they'd been crying.

'What's going on?' I said.

'Katriona, you can't stay here,' my dad said. 'We can't have a baby in this house.'

When he said that, and the way he said it, it was like being punched.

'I've nowhere to go,' I said, feeling like this was a bad

dream. They'd misunderstood something, surely? Why were they saying this?

'You'll have to find somewhere,' my mum said. 'There's too much going on in this house to have a baby in it.'

I knew what this was about. I'd been scolding everyone for leaving things around. I'd been saying things about the house being unsafe for a baby. I'd been on their case.

'I'll stop saying about the house,' I said.

'No, you're right,' my mum said, 'this house isn't right for a baby.'

My hands flew up to my chest. Was this happening?

'Where will I go?'

'No idea,' my mum said, 'but you have to go.'

'When?'

'Now.'

I looked at my dad. He stared and nodded. 'Now,' he said.

'Dad . . .'

'Don't want to hear it, Katriona,' he said. 'You can't stay here.'

My brothers followed me into the hall.

'Go to Fat Eamon's,' Michael said, 'it's empty.' Fat Eamon was a Scottish man who had run into some trouble and headed back home to Glasgow to get out of it. Around our way nobody ever told the council they were leaving. I stared at Michael. I couldn't believe he was saying that.

'Let me know if you can't get into Fat Eamon's,' he said.

I slept that night under a block of high-rise flats and the next day the boy broke into Eamon's abandoned flat in Stoneycroft Tower. When we kicked the door in it was in good condition: a small bedroom with a bed in it, curtains on the windows and carpets on the floor. There was a clean kitchen and table and chairs and a couch set.

Thankfully, the electric was still on. But I was scared, because I was fifteen, and as soon as I sat down on the couch the boy turned to me and said, 'I have to be home for my tea.'

I lived there alone for four months until a social worker found out about me and came to the flat.

'You cannot stay here and that's the bottom line,' she said.

'I'm fine,' I said. *Please help me.*

The social worker, Kay, had arrived a half-hour earlier, just as the party from the night before emptied out and went by her in the hall, leaving me – seven months pregnant – standing amongst the empty bags and cans and stinking ashtrays full of joint ends. She told me her name and job and that she was with child protection services. I thought she was talking about the baby, then I realized that I was the child who needed their 'protection services'.

She had come in with two council workers who had been round before. They knew I was squatting but I'd managed to get a few more weeks by insisting I was house-sitting for Eamon and he was coming back soon.

The place had become a drop-in for every teenager I knew and ones I didn't. Every night was party night and the locals had grown bored of it. They'd called the police and the council.

So I stood there, defiant. 'I want a flat, Kay,' I said.

Please help me.

She was suggesting a care home, a place for young mums, she said. I thought about Keresley Grange and the safety and warmth of it. I wanted this woman to put me in a taxi and send me there.

'I want a flat,' I insisted and stared at her with my arms folded across my bump.

Please help me.

Life there had become too much. The door didn't really close well, having been kicked in, so everyone and anyone could let themselves in and out. I had no money, no bene-fits, no support, and I relied on my boyfriend to feed me. I ate chips twice a day, down by the shopping centre where we still hung out. He never stayed with me in that place. Not once. I didn't blame him – I wouldn't have either if I'd had anywhere else to go. I couldn't go to his house, his mother lectured me if I did: this was all my fault, I had ruined her son's life. I think he really believed that too.

He and I, we were playing a game of life, not living one. He didn't have a genuine sense of responsibility for me or our growing child, we were an inconvenience. He felt no connection to the situation, why would he have? Society fed him the narrative that he had been trapped by a bad girl. His mother didn't think I was worth caring for and, well, my own parents didn't either, so why would he? I was an inconvenience, a stray dog in a shed. He came by when his friends wanted to smoke.

A few days before the social worker came I had been sitting in the squat when my boyfriend arrived with some of his mates, including these identical twins who knocked about with everyone, and I asked him to make me a cup of tea. He stood in the kitchen boiling the kettle and we were bantering back and forth in what I thought was good humour. He suddenly picked up the kettle and threw it across the room, over my head and through the balcony windows, shattering them.

'Fucking tramp,' he said.

I said nothing. This was real danger and I knew how to handle it. Eyes down, no reaction. The hot water had splashed down across my shoulder and neck when the kettle flew over me. I wasn't burned but it still stung.

The twins, who were sitting on the opposite couch, burst out laughing, and they clung to each other, almost as if they were trying to climb each other to get away from the fright.

'You mad bastard,' they said over and over in unison. My boyfriend, seventeen, just stood there staring at me.

One of the twins got to his feet. 'Come on, bruvver,' he said. 'Not getting me cuppa here, may as well go,' and they did. A few moments later my boyfriend left too.

I sat there for ages. I had missed a step and I couldn't figure it out. I didn't know what had happened and I was afraid of it. I got into the bed and tried to sleep, telling myself that I would wake up and I would be back at home and all of this would be nothing but a bad dream. I could go to school. I shut my eyes tight. I made myself sleep. But when I woke up I was still there.

What is going to happen to me?

The smashed window was clearly the last straw. Three men from the council came round. I told them Eamon was coming back but I hoped they didn't believe me.

So I was now standing with Kay in the middle of all the rubbish and dirt, and she was having none of it.

'You're not staying here,' she said.

'Flat, please,' I said. I was tiring myself out saying it, it was a circular conversation.

'Katriona,' Kay said, 'argue away, but you're a minor child and we cannot just leave you to your own devices, it's the law – I'm sorry but we are going to have to *insist* this time that you come to the hostel.'

Force me. Make me. Please don't leave me here.

'Well, I'm going to have to *insist* on a flat,' I said again, folding my arms and sticking my nose up at her.

'I can call the police, Katriona, to remove you,' she

said, fiddling with her folder and keys, 'or you can come now. We can see where we are in a few months, see how you get on with baby, and then we can look at getting you living on your own, look at getting you a flat.'

'I –' I interjected with no conviction.

Don't leave me here.

She frowned at me and gave me the sternest expression she could muster. 'Enough of that, come on, let's get going.'

Thank you.

'You're not going to drop it, are you?' I said. *Say no, say no.*

'No,' she said. 'Get your things, enough is enough, let's get you out of this –' she looked around – 'hellhole.'

I made an exaggerated sigh. Rolled my eyes wide.

'This is ridiculous,' I said.

Thank you.

'Let's go,' she said. She handed me a plastic bag.

'Oh, for God's sake,' I said, snatched it off her and took less than a minute pulling clothes off the floor and off the bed and shoving them into the bag.

As we left the flat the social worker had her hand on my back. I could feel the warmth of it through my shirt.

When John was born he was a squalling thing, blue and grey, and his head was misshapen, squashed into a point by the forceps they used to birth him. I thought my father's prophecy had come true and cried my eyes out.

My mother leaned across me and put her hand on the baby, stroked him and said, 'His head will go right in a while, it's just like that from the forceps.'

But I didn't stop crying. How had this happened? I wanted to be in the youth club with Louise, back working on that routine we had before all of this happened. I couldn't believe that there was actually a baby at all. Even though my stomach had grown exactly how it should, even though I'd gone through hours and hours of labour, the baby's arrival was a shock.

I ran my hand over his arms and legs, checked his toes and counted them. His fingers too. His face was bruised and swollen. I put my nose to his mouth and smelled his breath. The midwife came to take him for tests and I watched her like a hawk.

'What are you doing to him?' I said.

'Just two secs now, love,' she said, and I saw her stick a pin in his heel and press it with force on to a card.

'Why did you do that? Don't!' I said. I tried to sit up, tried to get up, but my legs were dead.

'She's just checking his blood,' my mother said.

'Now,' the midwife said, 'here he is, back to mummy.'

I looked at the baby, turned him over and traced his backbone. His nappy had folded back on itself. I fixed it.

My mum had been with me the whole time I was in labour. I had called the phone box across from our family house once I went into labour, hoping someone would pick up and I could get them to knock on our door. Luckily, my brother James did and told my mum.

Tilly nearly wasn't with me at all. A month before my son was born she had almost died. My parents were drinking heavily at that time; maybe without my presence there was nothing to keep things at bay. Anyway, they were self-destructing. One night my mother started to vomit blood, a varices bleed caused by a rupture in a vein from her destroyed liver. She was thirty-nine. She was in hospital for a month and barely survived it.

I went to visit her there but the toxins in her liver, unable to escape, were making her hallucinate and she didn't know it was me. Thankfully, she made it and discharged herself the day before I went into labour. I was glad, I'd have been on my own otherwise for sure.

'Your dad's moved out,' she said as I paced the floor with pains.

I didn't answer, convinced I was going to die as I hung on to the end of the bed and tried to breathe.

'I told him last night he was going to kill me if he didn't stop drinking or else he'd have to leave me,' she continued, 'so he left me.' She laughed then, shook her head. She had been sober and clean for a month. It was a mother I didn't really know. Her hair was darker and she was so thin from the illness she was almost unrecognizable. But it was this softness she had, this self-awareness, that was really unfamiliar.

Through the labour and the panic of it, as I tried to climb up the bed and get away from myself, my mum – free of toxins and addiction for the first time that I could remember – was urging me on, telling me I could do it. And afterwards when I had placental rupture and lost blood and they had to give me a transfusion, she never left my side. As I lay there recovering, she held the baby and kissed him and told him stories.

And as I fed the baby later when I felt a bit better, she leaned over and looked at his face as he lay in my arms sucking on his bottle, and she said, 'Come stay at home with me, all right?'

I remember this feeling flooding through me, like the room was full of sunlight, and even though the nurses were coming in and out, it felt like there was a bubble with me and my mum and this baby in it, and that was all I needed.

When we got home, we slept three in a bed. I remember the baby waking to be fed in the middle of the night and my mum woke too and there was this feeling of magic in the air, as if we had a secret. I felt like it was all going to be okay then, I felt like I could do it. Maybe I could go back to school.

It wasn't like that for long. My dad came home so I was back to the mother-and-baby hostel.

The hostel, Trentham House, was run by a charity called St Basil's. It was a small two-storey red-brick building. There was a reception and then a locked door that led to a kitchen area and staffrooms, and a staircase to where the mothers and babies stayed. There were maybe eight of us there.

We had freedom, and when I was pregnant and living there I still went every day to meet my friends at the Poolway. I went to my parents' house too and sat in the sitting room for a bit watching telly as people came and went. But in all that time I was in the hostel, which was close to a year and a half, nobody ever once came to visit me. That was hard for me to accept.

Mother-and-baby hostels are set up with this conflicting idea of supporting young mums while monitoring for bad parenting. Suspicion is not conducive to asking for support. When you are fifteen you think you should know instinctively how to look after your own baby, and nobody tells you that you won't. We never admitted we were struggling if we could avoid it. We saw lack of knowledge as being proof of the bad parenting we were being assessed for, so we hid mistakes or problems – admitting you weren't able was a step closer to getting your baby taken off you. And none of us wanted that.

When I see magazine articles aimed at older women, bemoaning the struggle of being a new mum, it makes me angry because I ask myself why being overwhelmed by the work of caring for a new baby is normalized for older mothers, but young mothers are punished for the very same thing.

The hostel was a pressured environment, with uniformed staff clucking in disapproval at you should you push the buggy through the doors later than baby's bedtime. They didn't know you'd missed the bus because your mother was drinking again, and you didn't want to leave her until your brother came home. They didn't know you were late because someone was in a good mood that day and acting like father of the year and you couldn't bear to take your baby away from that love bubble.

There is a pervasive attitude that young mothers do not feel real love towards their babies. That we have them to get flats or money or because we are lazy or vindictive. It's framed that way to dehumanize us because dehumanizing the most vulnerable is a great way to excuse yourself from helping them.

I loved my baby. I remember sitting on the floor of that tiny little room in St Basil's, with him leaning against the million teddy bears I had got him down the centre. I popped my head up, 'Boo!' And when his face broke into a huge smile, so did mine. He kept me going with that smile, that kid.

I was lonely and so I would hang around the kitchen longer than I needed, shaking bottles too long or fussing with the stuff in the fridge, so I might be still in there when someone else came in and I could have a chat. We were the misfits, the sluts, the bad girls, the gymslip mums, the scourge of Britain. We were full of bravado and none of us gave a damn. We wore our defiant faces all day. But in the mornings our pillows were damp and our eyes were red.

When my son was born, the hospital used prepared bottles and for the time you were in the hospital you could help yourself to the cupboard where they were. Nobody ever spoke to me about breastfeeding my son – not one nurse in the run-up to me having him, not one midwife afterwards. As I say: gymslip mums aren't *real* mothers.

When I was leaving the hospital, I filled an overnight bag with those little bottles. I knew you couldn't buy them, and I hadn't a clue how to make a baby's bottle. It was a solution. I must have taken a hundred of them. Every time my son cried, I took the plastic top off another one and fed him. I didn't really think about what would happen when they ran out. Then they ran out.

I remember standing there in the kitchen of the hostel with a bottle, a kettle and a huge tin of Cow & Gate baby milk that I had bought with my milk vouchers, which came as part of my benefits, and not having a clue what to do. I read the side of the tin, but it was written in a way that wasn't clear to me.

I knew I needed the nurse from downstairs to help me. This would be a black mark, I was sure of it. The nurses in St Basil's weren't the type of women I was raised around; they were the other kind. They wore a blue uniform and a uniform expression of disapproval. Except for one. The Irish one, Mary.

She came to the kitchen with me and I stood on the other side of the table from her and admitted, 'I don't know how to make it.' I braced myself. Readied for the lecture, the tutting, the eye roll, the scorn. These women were impatient with us.

Mary stood there for a moment and then she said, 'How would anyone know if they weren't shown?' and leaned across and pulled the lid off the tin. I was momentarily buoyed up by that. I lifted John from his buggy as he was starting to grumble and I swayed him on my hip. 'He'll probably cry now,' I said, 'but he's just hungry, he has a clean nappy.'

She looked at him. 'Well, isn't John a very lucky baby.'

She shook his little hand. 'Isn't mummy very good to you?' she said. I was surprised by that, but I felt really proud and I kissed John on his forehead.

She showed me how to scoop the milk powder and bang it on the side of the tin, and then to scrape it off with a knife. 'One per hundred mils,' she said.

I did it then.

'Brilliant!' she said. 'Isn't mummy clever?' she said to John. He blew bubbles at her and threatened a cry.

'Oh no,' she said, 'we better get this bottle cooled down!' She showed me how to run it under cold water a few times and shake it to get it just right.

'You're a natural,' she said.

That felt good.

'Any visitors coming tonight?' Mary said to me then and I pretended to think about it. The word *No* was overwhelming – if I said it, I might cry. So I shook my head.

She gave the bottle another shake and squirted some on her arm. John was starting to really complain.

'Well, after you've given him that bottle,' she said, 'come into the staffroom and bring him with you. I want to watch this show my sister told me about. She said it's a bit scary, so I could do with the company.'

'Oh, okay,' I said.

'Though you will get into it, it's supposed to be very good,' she said. 'So you'll have to put your Thursdays aside from now on to watch it with me.'

That sounded nice.

A little while later I was signed off as a capable mother and so the council gave me a flat and I left the mother-and-baby hostel. Mary came round on the first day with an enormous hamper full of everything I might need to start off.

My first flat was, funnily enough, back in Stoneycroft Tower in Bromford, where the squat was. It was sixty metres high, with twenty floors of flats, built in 1965 when the idea was that stacking the poor one on top of the other was a great space solution, freeing up the land for the rich to build mansions on. The truth was, those flats were like coffins in a mausoleum.

Stoneycroft Tower was demolished in 2011 and good riddance to it.

I had a flat a quarter of the way up. Coming from where I had, that tiny room in the hostel, I was delighted. I was sixteen.

When you move into a council place they give you a grant, so you can go and get the bits and bobs you'll need to live there. And I did. I was so thrilled with myself, I went into Birmingham and bought things I thought belonged in a proper home, a dark-wood-effect mahogany corner cabinet and a matching grandfather clock. Mary's hamper was full of knives and forks and cups with matching bowls and plates. There were tea towels and a tablecloth. I was so pleased. My son would have a real home.

The council had laid fresh carpet, and I vacuumed it every day, I did the washing-up and put the matching cups and plates back in the cupboards. I fluffed up the cushions and propped the baby up on the couch.

'Boo!' I said, popping my head up, and when he laughed I did too.

I was going to break the cycle, I knew it then and there on the fifth floor of that tower block. This little boy would have it all.

There are a few moments in my life when I could have been lost for good, pivotal moments that could have gone either way. If my father hadn't overdosed, if my mum hadn't gone out the day Bob came round drunk, if Sandra hadn't told on my dad in the caravan, if I'd never got pregnant, my life might have been quite different. And if I hadn't been at home the day Mr Pickering took a chance on finding me.

I was sitting on the floor coaxing my toddler to try to stand, the TV was on loud and I almost didn't hear the knock. But there was a flash of silence between ads and so I did. I opened the door.

'Sir!' I said it loudly, I was so surprised.

'Katriona, ah! I'm glad I found you,' Mr Pickering said, looking up and down the corridor. 'I tried a few of the . . . well, so, here you are.'

I stood there speechless, then realized I should ask him in.

'Come in, sir,' I said.

He stood the entire time, just inside my door, as I fussed and tidied up a little, trying to take in what it was he had come for.

'I came a few weeks ago, but I didn't know which number . . . it's just there is something I wanted to invite you to,' he said.

He told me he had arranged a part-time attendance programme at the school, so that I could come back for a couple of mornings and take English and maths. He had organized a small grant for childcare.

'You're a great student, Katriona,' he said. 'Please just do the GCSEs at least. That way you can decide later if you want to study.'

There was a moment where I wanted to say no. Just a flinch. Perhaps it was pride, or the knowledge that it would be really hard.

But then I looked over my shoulder at my son as he pulled himself up on his feet by the couch and I knew I had to go. I needed GCSEs. I wanted to go that far at least.

So, a few months later, I held my head as high as I could as I went back into school. All my former classmates were now doing their A levels. I'd see them on the corridors, but I didn't catch up to them. I let them walk ahead.

13

I managed to get my English GCSEs. But I was a kid living on my own and when it came to the second exam, maths, I just didn't go. I slept past the alarm. Still, at first, I tried so hard. I played house with my boyfriend and got a job in a cafe in town. He stayed at home on the PlayStation with the baby. At the weekends we partied, and all through the week we fought. We were too young, and then he left. And whatever I had been pulling myself up for went with him. If he didn't want *this*, maybe I didn't either. What was the point?

Being left to do it all alone, in a society that wanted me to prove myself time and time again, with no room for mistakes at all, was overwhelming. The legacy of my childhood made it a struggle to see my own value and gave me a hunger for reassurance that I was doing okay. Seeing myself as a useless single mother was only going to end one way.

I fell further and further through the cracks. My home became harder to keep tidy as I descended into deep despair. I gave up, stopped playing house, barely minded my son or myself. I couldn't stand my own company. My brothers or my dad came to take John every weekend and the minute they were gone I went straight out. That was where the men were, after all. I went out more and more, trying to find someone who would prove me wrong. Someone to tell me I was good, valuable.

The problem is that men who want sex will promise you the world. They'll tell you that you're the one, talk about holidays and marriage and you meeting their mother. They'll court you, for weeks, months. They'll swear it's forever, and then you never hear from them again. I fell for it over and over. Because there is no way to know.

What I should have been doing was staying home, reading or watching TV, while my son was in bed. But I had to find out, I had to know, was I worth anything to anyone?

And time after time after time the tape played out the same. I got a high every time I met the next Mr Right. And every time he stopped calling, I crashed. So, like any addict, you go harder. You get your fix. You go back and back again.

In Birmingham you can party twenty-four hours a day if you want to, there are clubs and pubs that run all day and night. The lower I fell in my own esteem, the more I turned to substances for a boost. I'd spend the weekends hanging out with whoever would have me, the music drowning out my inner voice.

Pissy pants, smelly, dirty child, trash, thick, mouth, sponger, waster, common, slut, slapper, bitch.

The more I abused myself, the stronger those voices got, the louder I wanted the music, the harder I went with the drink and drugs.

My best friends, Louise and Julie, stopped meeting up with me at all at the time.

Later I would go into recovery for drugs and alcohol, but the truth is, these were only ever a part of my problem. I went out into clubs and pubs and I boozed and took drugs because that was what was done there. I didn't want to find myself bored at home because in the quiet I felt like the real me. And she was a worthless piece of shit. That's what I got addicted to – escaping my reality and desperately seeking reassurance that I was worth something.

When my boyfriend left, I blamed everything on the flat. My parents had instilled a tradition of blaming your surroundings when things go wrong. So I couldn't stay there, and it was good timing. My dad had been arrested on a drink-driving charge and had made bail. He and my mum decided to skip it and go to Ireland. They could live with my grandad, who had been living alone in Clontarf since my granny had died a few years earlier.

We all wanted them to go. They'd never have survived

another sentence. My mum signed the family house on Blakenhale Road over to me. But moving in there, it infected me with its pain. Walking out of the door and seeing the Poolway right across the road, I was reminded of everything I'd been through.

I moved again, swapping with a girl I knew, to a house in Haydon Croft down by the Glebe pub. Things would be different there. I thought, as my parents had before me, that I could fix everything with a fresh start.

The house was clean, but I was not. I put some effort in, half painting the walls and doors, but I was not motivated. What was the point? I collected my benefits on a Monday and bought a token for the electric and gas – just one – and, the way I saw it, when that token was gone, it was gone. I had no reserves. Electricity and heat would usually be off by Thursday but it didn't matter – nothing did.

And soon the house would come to reflect how I saw myself. Trash. I recreated the childhood I'd had, drugs, strangers, mess. And in the middle of all of it, my little boy was trying to live. His life was chaotic and so was he. He missed his dad who – once things were over between us – never came round again.

I brought him to the doctor. I wanted help. I needed help.

'Can you get your son to sit down, Miss O'Sullivan?' the receptionist said. My son was bouncing off the walls;

he picked up a magazine and flung it. The pages came apart.

'John, sit down, please,' I said. The receptionist fixed me with a cold, hard stare. I felt like I was the worst mum in the world, even worse than my own, and I hated myself.

'Please stop him doing that,' the doctor said when I sat down and John didn't; he stood at her desk lifting whatever he could and moving things around.

'John, stop,' I said and attempted to pull him on to my knee, but he did that thing toddlers do where they drop their weight and he slid out of my hands. He screamed and kicked and knocked things over. He ran round the doctor's desk and grabbed the flesh of her forearm in his little nails and pinched, hard.

'John!' I pulled him back and he screeched.

'I'm so sorry,' I said to the doctor. She held her arm and rubbed it. And said nothing.

I tried to pick John up, but he bucked and screamed. I stood staring at the doctor.

Please help me.

The doctor just tutted and said, 'Please wait outside a moment, Miss O'Sullivan,' and so I did and then the receptionist told me I was to leave and not come back. I was barred from that surgery, she said.

My son deserved more in his early years. He deserved more than the broken mother and the unrest and fear that I know from my own childhood – he had that in abundance. I feel that guilt so deeply even now, but I do understand that I was wrecked. I don't mean tired when I use that word, I mean wrecked in the way a ship is when it hits the rocks. I was broken up, and parts of me were missing, and I was unable to breathe with the weight of the waves, constant, never ceasing. Crashing crashing crashing. The jagged edges of this hard life I had been given had ruined me. I had nothing and I had nobody and, living the way I was, that was the best I could do. I know that now.

One day my dad arrived at my door. He looked around and shook his head at the state of me and the state of the house. A sober hypocrite.

'I'm taking John back to Dublin,' he said.

'Okay,' I said and let him go.

I told myself this time on my own would be a chance to get it all together. I would sort everything, in no time, and John could come back to a lovely life with me. He deserved that. I could meet someone. My best friend, Louise, and all the girls I knew were in long-term relationships. They had no kids they had to collect or be home for. They kept saying I should find a nice man and come with them when they went out. It felt like a prerequisite to going to meet them at the pub, I couldn't go as a single.

'Find a boyfriend for God's sake, Kat,' Louise said.

I'm trying.

So I aimed low. I went down to the Glebe. The pub's gone now but it was a dive back then. A grey Victorian shithole. A place you'd never go. Drugs were dealt from there, arrangements for bad things were made there. The lowest of the low.

Someone like me could find someone there.

There was a gang of guys who drank there. I decided one of them was my type and so I went there every Friday and Saturday night to see him.

But it was another of that gang, Dan, who said he would walk me home. We had been drinking together in the pub and I'd been friendly because I liked the other guy so much. I agreed because I didn't want to look like I thought I was better than him. Even though I did.

Don't be rude.

And when he kissed me at the door and invited himself in, I made excuses that he ignored and tried to joke about it even though he wouldn't stop.

And even though I resisted, I never screamed for help. Even though he pushed me down and kissed me, even though I turned my head and said I was tired. Even when I laughed and tried to push him away playfully, he kept going.

'I don't want to go too far,' I said, and he pulled my top off. He lay over me on the floor.

Don't be rude.

When I said, 'Please, no,' he ignored me and put his arm across my neck and pulled my jeans off.

And then I said it: 'No, stop.'

But he raped me anyway.

And once again, I was seven and being suffocated by a man's body and by the shame of it, wondering what step I took that brought me here when I was just trying to live.

Why is he doing this?

I'd been asking myself that the whole way home, and at the door, in the hall and now here on the floor – how had he misunderstood me?

He didn't say anything after, he just stood up and fixed his clothes, and I fixed mine but didn't get up.

He stared at me and I knew he knew what he had done. He said night and left and I was crushed.

I was left again with the weight of this womanhood that I never asked for. This body that invited hurt and pain and shame just by existing.

After that, I wasn't well at all. I was so convinced I was bringing all of this on myself. The hole in my heart got so big that I got lost in it.

After the rape, I didn't want to go to the Glebe. I didn't even want to be seen in the area. I was afraid of Dan, afraid he would force me again. I rang my dad, I missed my son, and so he booked me on a bus to Ireland with the National Express.

When I got to my grandfather's house in Clontarf, with its painted houses and green spaces and the beautiful seafront, it was such a contrast to the brown and grey bricks of Bromford where I had come from. It felt like something, a sign. The air was fresh and there were no huge sprawling estates, not there anyway. There was a road with shops and a walkway and then the sea.

The house smelled like soup, and I could hear a kettle already boiling in the kitchen ahead of me as I came in the door. My gaze went to the hall table where a green phone, a vase of flowers and a bowl of keys sat. My parents were clean. My dad was sober.

'Where is he?' I asked my dad and he pointed to the living-room door.

'In there,' he said.

John was sitting on the floor with his back to me. His soft little shoulders were moving gently as he played with the figures he held in his hands, dancing them back and forth along the edge of the couch. He made action noises as he did, quietly under his breath. The silky football top I'd bought him six months before was now taut across his back – he had grown. He didn't hear me, he was immersed in the dialogue of his battle, and he laid his head on the sofa then, flying the figures up in the air and landing them down with a whoosh.

'Hiya,' I said, and he looked up.

He moved so fast into my arms and I was moved to

tears. I had never seen this side of my son before, this calmness. The wild brattiness was gone, he wasn't climbing the walls or destroying things. He was no longer the poster child for a dysfunctional gymslip mum. I felt jealous. Why was he so happy here, so peaceful? What did Dublin have that made my parents grow up and get sober and my son happy? It didn't feel fair.

I held John on my hip and his fingers rubbed the back of my neck like they always did when he was tired. There was material from Alcoholics Anonymous lying around, and not just one or two pamphlets – there were AA books and leaflets everywhere. My father always replaced one addiction with another.

I saw a Post-it note stuck to the mirror that read *Ask for help*.

'Dad!' I called, and he appeared from the kitchen. 'Can I come and live here for a bit?'

The problem had to be England. In England my parents were drug addicts, alcoholics, they were cruel and cold to me. In Ireland they were sober and good, kind and calm. I could see that from how they treated my son. I wanted some of that.

My dad said yes when I asked him if I could come over. He believed it too – everything would change in Dublin.

My mum and I went back to Birmingham together.

We planned to get my stuff and bring it back to Dublin and figure things out from there. I could stay in Clontarf for a while, find myself a flat if things worked out.

My mum didn't flinch when we went into my house, but I did. I saw the hellhole that I had been living in; the contrast with my grandfather's house that I had come from was stark. I felt ashamed of myself – I had been raising my son how I was raised. The place even smelled sour like my childhood home. Everything I thought I had been better than, I had become.

We dragged all that I owned into a pile and started bagging it up. After a while my mum groaned and straightened her back. 'I'd say there's a few heads down the Forester,' she said.

'Yeah,' I said, 'let's go for one.'

Five hours later we were on a dance floor in The Unit nightclub in Wolverhampton, off our heads. My mum's jaw was swinging. I couldn't focus on the guy she was talking to, did we know him? My mum's eyes rolled. *Shit.* She was out of it.

I told myself she was her own woman. She had charge of herself, nothing to do with me. She was the only person in control of her sobriety, and this had been her idea anyway. Nothing I could do. At the end of the day, she raised us this way, I was here because of her. It was her own fault.

Was it?

I've thought about this so many times, scrolled through images of my parents in my mind, settling on one and then the other as the villain of the piece. Who caused all of this? Was my mother the one, the Eve with a tempting apple, luring my dad into his bad behaviour? But I know better than that.

Because I am my mother. She is me. We are underclass women. That's a double oppression. She too believed her value lay in her worth to a man – she measured herself by whether my father loved her. That's the truth of it. The difference between us is that I had her as an example. I could learn from her mistakes. I wanted a better life for my kid.

By the time the weekend was over my mother had fallen off the wagon so hard she could barely speak. Neither could I. We lay around until we had to go, hung-over, drug-addled. It was no time to emigrate.

I don't remember packing, but I remember lugging a suitcase to the bus stop and waiting in a heap. I remember the relief of reaching Holyhead, the sea air fresh in my face as we made the crossing and left Britain and all the trouble behind us. Everything would be good in Dublin. I would be somebody in Dublin.

'Heading home or a holiday?'

I looked up to see a man standing beside me, smoking over the rails as the ship headed west. Handsome, I thought. Nice runners. Tattooed hands. My type.

'I'm moving to Dublin,' I said and flashed my best smile. Was this a meet cute? Was this the man of my dreams?

'Are you now?' he said, and held out his hand. 'Jay.'

'Katriona,' I said.

He looked me up and down a few times and smiled. The universal sign of interest.

I dropped my bags at Clontarf when we arrived, ignoring my dad's disgust as he realized we had been partying.

'Jesus Christ,' was all he said.

I had a cup of tea. My father looked down his nose, flaring his nostrils at my mother, who half hung off the table, in bits. After what I thought was an appropriate amount of time, about an hour, I headed into Dublin 1 to meet up with Jay.

Nothing would change in Dublin.

14

Rock bottom didn't look exactly as I'd imagined but I knew when I had hit it. I'd been in Dublin a few months and was slowly realizing that it wasn't Birmingham or my love life that was the problem. I was the problem.

I had come to Dublin to change my life and simply replicated it. I'd moved into a flat on Buckingham Street off Amiens Street in the middle of Dublin. I dropped John into my family in Clontarf on a Thursday and partied all weekend, just like before.

I was dating the wrong sort of guys, guys with all kinds of issues. Sometimes I'd meet one that was a good match for me, but as soon as they found out about my kid they would stop calling, or worse, leave me standing waiting under Clerys Clock. There is nothing that guts you quite like being stood up.

I kept looking at my parents, who were doing well in Dublin. Everything in my grandfather's house seemed so solid. I really wanted to join them in good living. My dad was a new person, full of good advice and an enthusiasm for sobriety that he never lost after that (even when he sometimes slipped off the wagon). Both of my parents were doing well.

But over and over I would find myself sitting in the middle of chaos, in the Blue Lion pub on Parnell Street where the smell of the men's toilets pervaded the entire premises. I remember looking around and knowing that not one of the people I was sitting with cared one bit about me. I knew they were there for the same reasons I was, for company, for something to do, for drink, and I could have been beamed up to outer space and nobody would even have noticed I was gone. I knew later we would head over to the city centre, find a club, dance all night, drink and do drugs. I knew none of it meant anything. It was a raging river on its way to meet an unpredictable sea and I knew it. I had to stop.

So one day – at the end of a hard weekend and my tether – I got the bus up to meet my dad and, over the course of a few hours, I told him my life story, how it was to be me. I told him about his overdose, being hit by the car, Bob. I told him about the boys, the joyriding, the times men had abused me. I told him about being on my own and the loneliness. I told him about the men who were still abusing me. I told him about my weekends, the men who stood me up, the benders, the drugs and drinks. How I would go and go and go.

I told him that sometimes, in my flat when I was there by myself, when my son was cosy and warm in his bed in Clontarf, I thought about him all night. I was no use to my son like this. His life with me was chaotic. I was a bad mum.

'Do you really believe that?' my dad said. AA had given him listening skills.

I nodded. 'When you took him over here, I couldn't control him. When I have him, I can't get through to him, he bounces off the walls,' I said.

'I'm really proud of you for telling me this, Katriona,' my dad said.

'I want a good life,' I said.

'I think you need to go into recovery,' he said.

The Rutland Centre is a rehab facility in Dublin. It's one of those places where people sit in circles speaking deeply about their addictions, where therapists scribble on notebooks as patients sit in silence, where the grounds are vast and full of trees, where everyone is there for the same reason: they are addicts who want to change.

I wanted to go. But I wanted to go there in the same way I had moved to Dublin, or Haydon Croft, or Blakenhale Road. I thought that I would fix myself up there and everything would be sorted. I didn't understand that I, Katriona O'Sullivan, would have to get to understand myself first, see myself clearly for the first time and open up. So when I went for the assessment interview the psychologist saw right through me.

'You're not ready to come here,' he said.

'What?' I was baffled, I had said *Yes* to every question. But I had my defences up.

'Take some time to think about what it is you might want from this treatment,' the guy said, 'and come back then.'

That was a shock. I stopped drinking and doing drugs and I returned for assessment ninety-two days later. They took me in then.

I'd love to say the Rutland Centre was an amazing experience and that it changed my life and made me see the reality of what I was doing, but that's not what happened. It was horrific, if I'm honest. I was this young thing who had learned to never talk and never tell. My whole life was spent keeping things on the down-low. I was supposed to keep the family secrets carefully guarded and now, in this weird open place, sitting in a circle with complete strangers, people wanted the truth. And I couldn't fool them. It threw me.

'Eoin,' the group therapist Pat addressed one of the men in the circle I sat in, day one, 'you've grown a beard. Are you hiding your face?'

Eoin didn't answer.

'What about you, Katriona? How are you?'

'Oh, I should have shaved before I came too,' I said. I expected laughter, but I didn't get it. The room was silent and serious, and I absolutely hated every single minute of it. There was no hiding, not for Eoin behind his facial hair, not for me behind a joke. I never got used to the group therapy.

There were family days, when your family would come and confront you with things you had done. My mum wasn't allowed, because at the time she was on medication for her addiction, and you had to be sober to partake. But my dad came up. I remember him sitting there speaking about how my behaviour affected him and I lost it. The cheek of him. The man who put me here out of pure selfishness and addictions that it seemed, now, he could have stopped anytime if he had wanted to.

I roared at him, 'How dare you say that? You ruined my life!'

But even though it was a hugely tough time I had some great experiences there, and at times I felt a freedom that I hadn't felt since I was a kid in school. I sang with a group during the centre's anniversary, in front of a crowd of people. In those moments, when I sing, I feel like my real self. The singer Frances Black came up to me after we finished, just as I was coming offstage, and she took my hands and said, 'Just sing your own song and you'll be okay.'

Things are really controlled in centres like that: what you watch, who you see and what you listen to. Music is controlled as it can have an effect on drug addicts;

something happens called a euphoric recall and it can lead to relapse. But we were allowed a stereo to listen to meditation tapes.

There were three young people there I warmed to, Paul, Jonno and Danielle. We hung out a lot and I started bringing the stereo up to the meditation room and putting rave music on. I thought nothing of it, I was used to breaking rules and being wild, rebelling against authority.

Then that Friday during our community meeting, when people would confront each other, Danielle said, 'Katriona keeps getting the stereo and playing music and it's affecting my recovery.'

'Oh my God!' I responded loudly. I was shocked that she was being so childish – in my view – and grassing on me instead of saying it to my face. 'You're supposed to be my friend, Danielle,' I said.

'You're supposed to be her friend, Katriona,' Paul said. 'You know she is an addict.'

'I'm an addict,' I said.

'And do you want to be?' Danielle asked. The whole room was staring at me.

'Uh, no?' I said. I sat back heavily and crossed my arms.

'Cop on, then,' she said.

It didn't have the right effect. I realize now they were trying to help me see what the differences are. But for me, it was as if I was being told I was a bad person. It hit core deep.

I lay in bed that night thinking about how they all clearly hated me, and I wanted to get away from them. I thought I had been making friends but now I felt like I couldn't make decisions, couldn't be trusted. I suppose in some ways it was worth it for that part. I know that sounds crazy, but being stripped of what you think you know makes you start at the beginning again. I was twenty-two and felt like I knew nothing.

Looking back, I can see my new path starting in the Rutland, because in many ways I didn't have any ideas about what I should or shouldn't be doing and I was open to being guided. And so when I met the people who would guide me through – the ones with ideas for me, the people who would support me and give me the tools to find my way to the gates of Trinity College – I let them.

Joe Dowling was a local man who ran a small community service centre by the Five Lamps in North Strand. It was a fantastic service for advice on benefits or where you could turn for training or a job. It was a hub. There was a great sense of community around where I lived in Summerhill. Through my short relationship with Jay from the boat I had got to know a few people. And through those people I got to know more people, and on and on. I was the 'English girl' to most. I felt a community begin to support me.

In the late nineties, there was plenty of money in Ireland. So people in crisis, the poor and the troubled, had a lot of services if they needed them. (Of course, these services were stripped back over the years, after the crash. The poor are always the first targets for budget cuts.)

Joe knew everyone, politicians and elected representatives, heads of departments, lawyers, teachers, and who to call and where to go to get sorted. It was a great service.

'I just don't know what I'm doing,' I said one day after popping in. There was a cup of tea in my hand and Joe was shuffling through his diary, looking for a number.

'You should talk to someone,' he said, 'figure that out, with help.'

Joe was a great believer in help.

'And I'm still single,' I said. It was a lament.

'Get a nice fella for yourself,' he said in sympathy.

'None of them want me, Joe!' I said.

'Maybe you should talk to someone about that too,' he said. He found what he was looking for and dialled a number. 'Marian? Joe Dowling here. I have someone I'm sending up to you, a lovely girl who needs to chat to you.'

He hung up. 'Now,' he said, writing out an address on a notepad, tearing the page out and handing it to me.

It said *Oasis Counselling Centre, Sherrard Street, 11AM Wednesday.*

There is something so necessary about safe spaces. For people like me there aren't enough of them. I'd found one in Mrs Arkinson's class, and in Keresley Grange, and in the kitchen of our youth club with Mel, and in the school office with Mr Pickering. And now, again, I found one in the Oasis Centre.

A safe space, for me, is somewhere that I can speak freely, from the heart, and tell my truth without the fear that I will be challenged or shown up, or that something will be taken or stopped or changed. Those places are so necessary, especially for people like me.

When you are raised by addicts in an unsafe environment like I was, where adults are unpredictable and dysfunctional, you become hyperaware. Mistrust becomes a tool of survival. I suppose all animals have this instinct when they need it. You might imagine a mammal born in a place teeming with snakes, over one born where there are no snakes at all. The first one would flinch when the grass moved, right?

I flinched. Whenever I met anyone in authority, I was instantly suspicious, instantly mistrustful. I flippantly call that my 'bullshit meter' but it is actually a safety meter.

Are there snakes here?

When I got to the Oasis Centre I checked for snakes. I sat in silence with the therapist, Marian, for a long time. But then, after a few weeks, once I saw the grass was still, I started to talk a little, and I felt safe there.

And the safer I felt, the more the floodgates opened, and I would leave the centre every week with red eyes, a sore throat and a heart that was stitching back together. I talked and talked and talked.

Sometimes about really little things, like the way someone had spoken to me, or something someone did.

Sometimes I hated my parents and wished they would disappear.

Sometimes I loved my parents and wanted them to have their lives over.

Sometimes I was a bad mother.

Sometimes I was the best mother in a bad situation.

I loved myself, I wanted more.

I hated myself, I didn't deserve anything better.

All the changing tides of how humans feel and think were channelled from my heart into that space and they sat there, unjudged and safe. And at the end of every outburst, every story, was my champion.

'Well, he sounds like a right fool,' Marian would say about whoever it was that had upset me.

'Well, it does sound as if you really like him,' she would say about the same person next time, when I'd changed my mind.

Unwavering support influences self-esteem. It had – still has – a huge effect on me. To be able to speak my truth, without fear, to spill my guts, and instead of being faced with rejection, scorn and shame, to be held up, supported and championed instead? It makes all the difference.

People dread therapy because they think of scenarios like the Rutland Centre, spaces where you feel stripped bare and humiliated, and I understand that. I never want to go back to an environment like that. It has a purpose: they break you down and make you so open you can't hide from your demons at all. It's a road to recovery for people with addictions and it has a proven track record. But what I needed was someone to listen so I could find my own way. I didn't have walls to break down, I needed walls built up to support me.

I needed encouragement to build my life and the tools to give it structure and strength. I needed tools to understand the world and how to think.

I needed education.

15

I came out of the Rutland determined never to drink or do drugs again. I was never fully sold on the idea that I was a drug addict. Yet I was also still bouncing around the clubs and pubs, on a search for a partner. I avoided being at home as much as I could, leaving John with my dad and going to AA meetings. It was my social life.

I don't want to say I was too young to be a mother. Plenty of young women make excellent mothers. And I was a loving mother, I'll say that for me. But I was too young to handle everything I was dealt at that time. It wasn't the child; it was the whole lot. It takes time to fix twenty-odd years of absolute mayhem. Everything that I felt about myself in Birmingham, I still felt in Dublin. I don't think I had ever had a healthy relationship, not with a man or even in my platonic female friendships, until I moved to Dublin and got into recovery and therapy. I had no confidence, though. My friendships were good ones, but I was always waiting for things to fall apart.

I spent the first two years in Dublin going from one

man to the next. All similar, none of them suitable or available for a relationship. I was so young, trying so hard to find a place for myself, a sense of belonging maybe, and I was taken advantage of by people for that. I met Mikey, a good-looking guy who saw me only on Saturday nights. When the club closed he would come and find me and come home with me. By the next morning he would be gone. I went to the nightclubs every week, danced as if I was having the time of my life, but watched him chatting to his friends and having the craic on the other side, wishing the club would end so he would take me home and hold me.

I would spend my week dreaming about a life with him, where we would have a little council house and nights out at the pub and holidays together. But every weekend I'd just get that same treatment, and I didn't push it – I never asked for more, I just went along with it. Because maybe those few hours of love, or what felt like it, got me through.

I pretended I was an empowered woman. I let on to Mikey that all I wanted was the same as he wanted, but it wasn't. I told myself that I had the power, but I didn't. Eventually he started walking past me in the club and I went home alone.

Talking to Marian about all this every week was doing something to clear up my headspace, and I was starting to identify certain things that could change. But it was going to take something more profound than a therapy session to put me on the path to real recovery. I was looking in the wrong places for a partner because I didn't believe I had worth.

A friend, Derek, lived in a house share on Dorset Street. I was always up banging at the door, looking for him to hang out, ignoring the other guys who rented rooms there, Dave and Paul, working men who had nice cars and nice mams. They'd stop to talk to me, offer me tea, and I had no interest in them. I stayed away from nice guys. I wasn't valuable enough to trade my company for their affections. I set my sights low.

Being a young mum is such a lonely place, especially when everyone around you is free to be young, and you're stuck. You get into these friendships based on the other person's terms, because you get something you need – company and fun – and it seems like a fair exchange. So I compromised.

Derek was fun, always bopping around town with a ghetto blaster, having the craic. He liked me, but I didn't fancy him at all. It seems crazy now but at that time in my life I was so vulnerable I didn't think it was up to me to decide what was or was not for me. So when Derek wanted to sleep with me, I went along with it. We started sleeping together casually, for 'fun', but Derek had issues and so did I, and again, that fizzled out.

*

About a year after leaving the Rutland, I made a new friend, Audrey. She was the kind of person to see right through you, to know right away where you were going wrong and to tell you. She was exactly what I needed, exactly when I needed it.

'What are you doing here?' she would say to me after our AA meetings, when I would hang around or go for coffee, knowing my son was at home with my dad. 'Don't you have a child to be minding?'

I always brushed her off. 'He's grand,' I'd say, and I wouldn't go home. I was avoiding the loneliness. It was in the alone times when my inner voice was loudest.

'Go home, Kateria,' she would say then, never getting my name quite right, 'that's where it is, what you need.'

'Oh yeah?' I said. 'What do I need then?'

'Peace,' she said.

Eventually that routine wore me down. I started to listen.

Peace? At home?

Yes.

How?

It's where your son is, that's home.

I can't connect with that place, I don't know how to. It feels like I'm going mad in there, like I'm going to die.

Find one thing, connect with your son on one thing, and you'll be okay.

One thing. That day, when she said that, I replayed it over and over in my head as I walked up to collect my son from school. *One thing.*

What thing?

'Hey, Katriona!' My neighbour, Joe Dowling's son David, was standing out in front of the shop. I never bumped into David.

'How's things?' he said.

'Ah, same same,' I said, 'you know yourself.'

'How's the young fella?' he said, and I said fine.

Then he said, 'Loves the football, doesn't he?'

'He does love the football, David,' I said. I wasn't exaggerating. I used to dress John in Manchester United tracksuits all year round to keep him happy. He was known as the English kid with the football in Summerhill.

'Yeah, I thought so,' David said. 'I do always see him out there with the ball morning, noon and night. You know, Belvedere are having trials tomorrow, down the park?'

When David told me about the trials, it felt like destiny. What Audrey had said and now this. It felt like alignment. I knew right then that me and John would be at those trials, I knew he would get in, I knew that every single week, rain or shine, I would be there supporting my son.

I had, for the first time in Dublin, a real focus. I thrive when I have a focus, and Audrey could see that in me and knew I needed one. She calls it being 'on the beam', those times in life when you just know you are on the right track, and you feel so good for it. Watching my son playing football every week was that sort of feeling. Because Audrey was such a force for good in my life, I really wanted to be around her, so I would deliberately pass her flat after dropping my son off at school and go to the phone box, where I would call and see if she fancied tea. She always did.

'You've brains to burn,' she told me over and over. I loved hearing that.

'Sure, what good are brains to me?' I said.

'All I know is I've never met someone as clever as you, Kateria,' she said.

I shrugged. People like me didn't do anything with brains, except scam, and I didn't want to do that.

From my early days in Mrs Arkinson's classroom, I had believed I deserved more, but I didn't really know what 'more' was. By the time I reached my late teens, I would have told you that I wanted my own council house, secure benefit payments and to make sure my son, John, was happy and had what he needed. But even when I had those things, house, benefits, like I'd had in Birmingham, I was miserable.

And when I came to Dublin and eventually got the offer of a council flat, near people I knew, I refused it. I still wanted more, but the path to exactly what – or what more was – that was never clear.

I was convinced of my 'place' in society and I believed that my place was with the underclasses, getting my one-parent payment – which we called our 'book' due to the way it was sent out to us in a set of bound money orders – on a Thursday, paying the few bills when I could, cooking frozen food for my son and getting him the good runners. I was looking for a man – it was going to be the fix-all solution, someone I loved, who would love me and who would love my son. I dreamed that we would go to the pub sometimes, the pictures, or even on a sun holiday together.

But I did have ambition. I wanted to find a way to not have to answer to the social welfare. It always felt like I was being watched over my shoulder. They give you barely enough to cover the week, and never enough to live easy, but if you get any opportunity to earn some spare cash, you have to hide it or they will take it back. You are forced into this game of cat and mouse, and it wears you down. Single parents cannot survive without cheating the system to give their kids any semblance of a good childhood, and they are the ones most often punished for it.

At one point I was cleaning toilets in Connolly Station for cash, leaving my sleeping son and running over the road to wipe counters and seats and empty bins, and

I remember thinking *Is this why I am on earth? To clean piss off seats? What am I here for?*

At that time the social welfare always encouraged us to do courses and schemes, and most people did as it didn't affect our payments, and these schemes got people on the road to work. The country was full of money at that time, and it was trickling down into the working classes.

'You've brains to burn, I'm telling you,' Audrey said.

'Doesn't matter, does it?' I said.

'Yeah, it does,' she said. 'Just you watch.'

It's funny because even though I never considered going to college, I was heading that way. College had never come into it because nobody I knew ever went to college. But, somehow, I was being pushed and pulled in that direction. What drives me in any situation has always been the desire to be 'better'. It would have been so easy to go down the same road my parents had; it was expected by everyone, wasn't it? But I wanted to go on my own road. Like Frances Black said, I would sing my own song. I just didn't know the tune yet.

I signed up for a parenting course, determined to give my boy the best start in life. The Larkin Centre was on the North Strand in a grey Georgian house with steps up to it. The door was painted in navy blue, similar to the colour of the social welfare logo. In a weird way, that made it less intimidating.

I had forgotten what it felt like to learn. I guzzled the

information, learning about nutrition and the way the body took in food. Until that course, I really believed that pizza and chips was a good dinner. Nobody had ever told me otherwise. Now, I was learning about the food pyramid. I loved the classroom element, the sitting in rows with a notebook. I was comforted by the familiar feeling of it: *I'm supposed to be here, I belong here – my name is on the list.* Sitting in a classroom, taking in the information, the atmosphere of learning. I was on the beam.

'. . . it converts the starch to sugar in the blood,' I told Audrey, explaining to her what I had learned.

She stared at me. 'Brains to bloody burn,' she said.

In those days, with funding the way it was, your benefits weren't affected by doing a course through the VTOS or CE Scheme*, and you could get grants and payments to cover childcare. Once I'd done the parenting course, and caught the bug of learning again, I started to look around for the next thing.

There was a theatre course running in Ringsend. I thought about the joy I'd felt when I performed in *Dianella* and the Rutland Centre show, and I realized this was exactly what I wanted.

The course ran from 9.30 and so I would drop John to school and rush over. There were only mature students

---

* Vocational Training Opportunities Scheme and Community Employment Scheme

on the course, but I was the youngest along with a guy called Thomas. Within a few weeks, despite the age differences, the small group of theatre students had bonded. I loved it and time flew.

That little gang in college, an eclectic mix of people, all outgoing personalities with huge creative energies, all wanting to learn, was exactly the medicine I had needed. I felt a strong sense of place there, of worth and value. A place to express myself, to be myself, to shine. It didn't matter my mood, once I went there, I found support on every level. The small blocks of self-esteem shuffled into place and my feet started to find solid ground again.

'How about the Seven Deadly Sins?' I said to my little group. We were making a film and I could not contain myself. I was thriving.

'Like greed and all that?' Thomas said.

'Yeah, like greed, envy, laziness . . .' I said.

My friend Margo said, 'Sloth?'

'That's the same as lazy,' I said. 'The others are pride, gluttony, wrath and . . . oh, it's . . . um . . .'

'Vanity!' Margo said.

'I think that's a brilliant idea, let's do it,' someone else said. Everyone agreed.

'I'll be lust,' Samuel said, rubbing his thighs and licking his lips, leaning against Trish, who was the oldest person on our course.

'Get off, you,' she said and pushed him. He fell

dramatically out of his chair and lay on the floor. He folded his arms.

'Sloth it is,' he said.

'Gerrup!' Margo said. 'Right! Who wants to do the camera?'

I threw my hand up.

'Katriona, surely you should be on the other side of the camera?' Thomas said, and I noticed he blushed. 'You should . . .'

I shook my head; I didn't want to act. This course had taught me that fact quick enough. I didn't like being directed, I had to be the one in control.

As we walked down the road a few days later to film our dailies, Thomas caught up with me.

'Have you plans for the weekend?' he said, and cleared his throat, swallowing hard. 'There's a —'

'Yeah, I've loads on,' I cut him off. He was too sweet — kind and soft, not my type.

I turned round. 'Margo, you should direct, it'll be good for your CV,' I said, and she ran up to me and took the script.

We filmed everything and went back to the editing room. I was exhilarated by the creativity; it was making me giddy. I bounced back into class.

The teacher looked up. 'Katriona, there was a call for you. Your dad needs you to call him back.'

*

'Katriona,' my dad said down the phone.

'Yes, Dad,' I said. My stomach sank.

'Your mum . . . she crashed the car again,' he said. 'You have to go to the hospital.'

I closed my eyes. *Typical*.

'How bad?'

'Pretty bad, but can you go because I have to find a meeting. I swear I need it.'

'You're not going to the hospital? Dad, I'm on an assignment . . .'

'I might drink . . . I need a meeting.'

Every time.

'Okay, Dad, I'll go.'

'That's my Katriona,' he said.

My Katriona. I hated that now.

I thought about the class, making their film without me. I was irritated and tired of all of this. It was like I could not move forward without my parents reaching out and grabbing my ankles, determined to pull me back down with them. My dad was sober, why was he not the one going to support his wife? Why could he not let his daughter grow? Why was it always me?

My mum was fine: broken arm, broken rib – but fine.

'This is the eighth time, Mum,' I said.

My mum was in constant trouble, she could not quit her addictions. She and my dad were fighting all the time.

She was in AA and really trying. But she just couldn't figure it out.

And it was getting harder to be in that triangle, with my dad on one side and my mum on the other, both reliant on me, both getting in my way. I wanted education, to be on the course, working with others and meeting deadlines and using my brain. I was growing and I could see a path appearing through the fog already.

By the end of my theatre course I knew I didn't want to be an actor and I didn't want to be in show business. I had learned so much but that was the most important thing, I knew what I didn't want to do. And so, when the course ended, in many ways I was back to square one. But it didn't matter. Back then, trying things, for people like me, held no shame. You could hop from course to course.

Ironically, not long after that, a girl I knew told me about a job in the Institute of Education, an expensive grind school attended by middle-class kids to maximize their chances of getting into the best university courses. Single mothers in poverty are jacks of all trades, we take the jobs that fit in with our children and career paths have nothing to do with it. We need the money. The job was cash in hand, working as a dinner lady in the small canteen there, serving sausage rolls to the kids enrolled.

In those days I had a blanket idea that everyone in education past secondary school was rich. That was my belief. So the kids in the Institute were 'poshies' that I had nothing in common with at all. I played the music I liked on the canteen radio and ignored them. I was only five years older than most of them, but they didn't see it that way and neither did I. To me, they seemed to swan in and out in designer loafers with expensive school bags while looking fashionably unkempt. To most of them I was a domestic or a servant, patronized and sympathized with at best.

I didn't have any interest in these kids. I didn't care who they were. They were the ones on the other side from me, who had what I never had. It didn't enter my head that any of them had hard lives, because I judged them on where they were, not what they were coming from.

'I miss having something to do, college was great,' I said to my friend Ashley, sitting in my flat. 'I'd love to do a course again.'

'You're mad,' she said, 'stick with that job, it's grand.'

I shook my head. 'I might see if there's another one going on somewhere, maybe a scheme.'

'They're gonna take that book off ya,' she said, shaking her head too and whooshing her baby higher on to her knee, planting a kiss on the crown of his head. 'You'd be lost without your book, Katriona.'

16

My grandfather died that year, in 2001. My mum and dad had been living with him, and both were sober at the same time for the first time in years. My mum told me she had a sponsor, a woman named Anne, and was staying away from alcohol. Things were quiet.

My dad returned from the hospital after my grandad died, really shook. And he told us the story about his origins that he had learned for the first time – that the nun he had known as his aunt was actually his mother. At first, we weren't sure what to think. Tony made up a lot of things. But the depth of his turmoil over it all made us believe him.

Tony had been sober for a long time but he became unstable. We thought it no wonder: in one swoop, it seemed, he had lost his father and found his mother too late for it to make any difference since she was dead. But my dad was playing some kind of mind game – maybe even with himself.

'What's wrong with you?' I asked my mother down the phone. I could hear she was crying.

'Your dad is definitely seeing someone else, Kat,' she said, and I rolled my eyes. Here we go.

'Don't be ridiculous.' I was stern. I wasn't up for the drama.

'He went away to Donegal,' she said. 'Supposed to be on some AA thing, but nobody has heard of it.'

'He *is* gone to do that, stop,' I said.

'Ring him for me, will you?' She begged me, wouldn't let it go. So I did.

I knew the minute my dad answered the phone that my mum was on the right track. It was the way he answered and the way he spoke to me like we were strangers. My stomach sank. He was with someone else.

I asked him straight out.

And he answered me straight out.

'Yes,' he said, 'I'm here with Anne.'

'Anne? Anne who? Not Anne Murphy? . . . *Dad?*'

'Yes,' he said.

Jesus Christ.

'Dad, that's Mum's sponsor,' I said.

'Well,' he said, 'we —'

'You're disgusting!' I said and hung up.

I called my mum back, told her my dad was going to come over to talk to her and told her nothing of what he'd said to me. Not out of loyalty at all. I couldn't possibly have found the words.

I watched TV for the evening, distracted, waiting to hear from my mother. She never called and I avoided the temptation to check in. I was so angry at my dad.

So when my phone rang at midnight, I knew it was something. My heart stopped, of course, and I knew it wasn't going to be good.

I grabbed my phone off the counter, reaching for my box of smokes and lighter as I said, 'Hello?'

'Is this Katriona O'Sullivan?' a man asked, west of Ireland accent. It was the gardaí.

'Yeah?' I said.

'Your father is Tony? Your mother Tilly O'Sullivan?'

'Yeah?' I said.

'There has been an incident,' he said, and I sat straight down on the floor.

My mother had stabbed my father in the head.

I have run through hospital doors enough times to do me for a lifetime. It's the most out-of-control feeling you can experience, and that night was the worst. On all levels I was terrified. My mum had stabbed my dad. It was a hard thing to take in. I was so angry – at him for causing her such a dark level of pain that she would do something so *horrific*, and at her for being so violent and *stupid*. Angry at both of them for always dragging me into the shit. But once you run through those doors and see the person you are running to, anger turns to anxiety. Perhaps the two aren't so different.

My dad was okay: the knife had gone through his skull but avoided, luckily, anything important. It was a relief.

The anger hit again and I called him names under my breath as I sat in the corridor. I decided that *he* had caused all of it. It was his fault. I was fuming. But later, when I picked my mother up from the garda station where she had been arrested, I decided *she* had caused it.

My mum was going to have to stay with me as the gardaí wouldn't let her go home. So when my dad was released from the hospital, he went back to Clontarf with his new woman. My mum's sponsor.

Getting my mum back to my house, she went straight down to the pub. It was not unexpected. When she finally came home and slept it off, she woke the next morning really upset with herself and my dad and apologetic.

'I'm not gonna go drinking again,' she said.

I believed her.

My dad would not have my support. No way. If he was with another woman, he was on his own. The story I had was that my tiny vulnerable mum had given Anne her trust, confided in her, asked her for support and help, and had been – as I believed – betrayed. I felt deeply disturbed and deeply wounded by that betrayal. I didn't care that Anne was an alcoholic, struggling with addiction. I didn't want to know what she was going through that made her stoop so low, I wanted her nowhere near me and nowhere near my family.

I told my dad that my son was to go nowhere near

that house, and when I found out he had taken him there I went up and banged the door down. I was not having anything to do with this, I screamed. I stopped speaking to my dad. Now he was the one on the outskirts of the family. He was the black sheep.

We found my mum a little cottage in Cork Street, in the south inner city, and it was the best year for her since she had met my dad. She was connected to me and John, we talked so much, and she explained herself. It was the same mother I'd had in my last weeks of pregnancy and as a new mother. This was Tilly-without-Tony and she was so full of care and realness, I thought we would be okay.

But whatever magnet had forced this collision of crazy, my parents' connection was too strong. She couldn't resist him, bogged down by the same set of institutional rules that every woman is, the ones that say you must stand by your man. If he is happy, you are happy too, he comes first. Tony, on the outskirts, out of contact with me and his adored grandson, wanted to come back.

'Your dad wants to go for a coffee,' my mum said.

'With who?' I was confused.

'Me,' she said.

My stomach sank.

'Mum, you're doing so well,' I said. I held her hand. 'Please don't go, it's not a good idea.'

But I knew she would go. I knew she would go, and

he was drinking and so she would drink too, and her good streak and happiness would be over. I knew she would be back crashing cars and making my life a misery. And I was so angry I could barely express it.

I always saw my parents as drowning, pulling each other under. One would be doing well and the other would find a way to get them back down to the bottom. It's why the AA advises people to cut ties with everyone and begin again, not to go to places you used to drink, not to see people who drink. It sounds easy – if someone really wanted to be clean they would do it, right?

But what if your shared identity is important? What if the person you are depends on the other? What if what you belong to, where you feel at home, is this pit of despair? Maybe your loved one is down there and so you want to be too. I learned years later that humans form strong connections with their environment, so much so that the environment becomes part of the behaviour itself. In the way we remember how to ride a bike, the automatic response to environment clicks in just like that, so addicts who come back together have an urge to recreate that environment. It's an automatic behavioural response in motion. I knew that, not from education but experience. I knew that this casual meet-up would lead my mum back to drinking and her life spiralling out of control once again.

And I was right. More than ever, I wanted out of all of this. I just wanted my own life. I wanted something big, but I couldn't put my finger on what it was or where to get it. That was to change.

I hadn't seen my friend Karen in ages so when I saw her crossing O'Connell Bridge, I stopped her to say hi. She wasn't surprised to see me, and of course she stopped to chat.

Everyone knows everyone in town.

We stood on the median together.

'What are you up to?' I said to her.

'I'm in Trinity,' she said. 'I'm studying law.'

My heart started to pound in my chest.

'No way, Karen,' I said.

Karen was a townie through and through, brought up in abject poverty in the city centre, like me, and a single mother, like me. Her dad was Joe Dowling, the wonderful man who ran the little centre in North Strand, where I used to call in all the time for support.

'What are you doing?' she asked.

'I'm working in a canteen,' I said, waving the question away with my hand to get back to the reason my adrenaline was spiking. 'What do you mean, you're in Trinity?'

She took a minute to light a cigarette and put her bags down between her feet.

'Yeah,' she said, 'I'm studying law.'

'Law? Like *law* law?' I was baffled by this. 'In Trinity College like?' I pointed at it, the grey walls and buildings in view from where we stood.

She nodded, took a drag. 'Yep.'

'How the . . . ?' I felt something stir . . . Was it jealousy?

'I did the access programme there,' Karen said. 'It's for girls like us, Katriona. You go in and learn how to go to college, and at the end you can pick your course for a degree.'

'For real?' I said. 'Ah here, Karen, they'd never let me in the door of that place.' I tried to joke, but I could barely hear myself over the pounding of my heart. A beam of sunlight had lit the street.

'How did you get on to it?' I said. I put my purse back in my jacket. Penneys could wait.

Trinity College was a landmark, somewhere lads I knew went to rob bikes. I never looked at it when I passed it, never thought about what was going on in there. I didn't care about its history or what it stood for. There was nothing for me in there.

So my dreams were limited – I didn't have anyone talking about college around me, nobody ever mentioned it. In school, the teachers hoped kids like me would make it to do the GCSEs and go on to a trade. In poor areas like ours, kids were encouraged to do hairdressing, childcare and catering, not history, politics or maths.

Years later, I would argue against the corralling of poor kids into trades and low-level careers and be shocked to my core at the widespread belief amongst educators that those born into poverty lack the brains for third-level education. I fight this nonsense every day.

On O'Connell Bridge that afternoon, Karen explained to me how she got into Trinity. She started at the beginning, told me about the Trinity Access Programme, how people like me could apply to do a course where you'd be helped to go to college. She said she loved it, told me it was brilliant, said there was loads of support and the people running the course were great.

'I'd love to do something like that, Karen,' I said.

She dropped the end of the cigarette and stood on it.

'And they pay you,' she said. 'You get childcare and all.'

I wanted to pinch myself. The ground under my feet was turning to gold.

'Where is it on?'

I'd love to see a video of myself marching over to Westland Row that day. I could not move fast enough. I was a woman on a mission. For the first time in my life, I knew where I was going. I was going to Trinity.

There was a security guard on the door to the building around the back of the campus, across from the Dart Station. I asked him to show me where to find the

Trinity Access Programme and so he pointed me to a door with a glass window. I knocked and looked in the window and the lady in there glanced up and waved at me like she knew who I was.

'Hi!' she said and beckoned me to come in. She had a small, stern face under a mass of brown curls. I pushed open the door.

'Hiya,' I said. 'So, my name is Katriona O'Sullivan and . . . I want to go to college . . . I know Karen Dowling and I just met her and she told me she goes here – how is she going here because I want to go here –'

She smiled widely at me, introduced herself as Irena and said, 'Would you like to sit down?'

I shoved myself on to the chair. *Come on come on let me in let me in.*

'It's just –' I said, 'Karen Dowling is a single mother, I'm a single mother as well, and I want to go here, so when she told me – look, how can I go here? I want to go here.'

I felt like I couldn't speak fast enough.

'You want to do the access programme here?' Irena said. 'Why?'

Why?

How could I ever explain? How could I speak on my life in a way that would even touch on the depth of why I wanted out of it?

Where I lived, my lot was considered a good one: I

had my payment every week, I had my rent paid, I had my little job, the few bob on the side. I'd find a nice fella soon, right? I'd eventually get a council flat next door to a friendly face, what was wrong with that?

Nothing.

It just wasn't what I wanted, not for me and not for my son. It wasn't enough for me.

'I want . . .' I let the air out of my lungs that I'd been holding in since I'd met Karen. I looked around the room.

Irena stayed quiet. She gave me a nod.

'I want to know everything,' I said.

'Everything?' Irena raised her eyebrows.

'Yeah, everything,' I said.

She tilted her head and narrowed her eyes. 'Do you read, Katriona?'

'Oh yeah,' I said, being fully truthful. 'I love reading, I read everything, actually. I had this teacher, years ago, before I left to have my son – I had him when I was sixteen – but anyway, this teacher I had . . .' I told her the story of Mr Pickering and about the books, I told her about my parents, the drugs, the care home, the dress I got from Mrs Arkinson, and I told her about the squat, the flat, the drugs, the loneliness, the stress. I sat there for an hour and gave her the entire scene.

'. . . and I just want to come here,' I finished.

We sat for a minute in that pause and then she said,

'Well, aren't you amazing?' I felt a surge of energy from those words. 'Katriona, I would love you to apply for this course.'

Phew.

'How do I do that?' I said. I wanted the form, I wanted the pen. I wanted *this* – this office, this woman, this feeling. I wanted books, and Trinity, and somewhere to go every day; I wanted out of my bedsit, my loneliness, my heartbreak, my pain.

'Go home and write your opinion on a news story, something current. I want you to give me your honest opinion about it, write it out and hand it into this office on Friday marked for my attention.'

'Okay, yeah, I will.' I wanted to start right away, so I stood up to leave.

'Read through these as well,' she said, handing me pamphlets.

'I will,' I said, and I left. And this time I turned right instead of left and I walked up around by the railings of Trinity College. I stopped and stood up on my toes to look over to the green. I could see students walking around and some sitting in groups on the grass.

That's me, I thought, and I knew it was true.

I got an interview. I was sure that meant I was going to Trinity, so I was delighted with myself. When I went for the interview there were a few others waiting outside.

I had a folder on my lap filled with the information that Irena had given me on Trinity and the Trinity Access Programme (TAP). It had been designed, the leaflets said, for early school leavers, for people who had chosen other paths like trades, or for people who simply never took that route. The course would work like a taster menu for college subjects, and it would teach you how to write an academic essay, how to meet a deadline and overall prepare you for a degree course in Trinity. I had read everything twice. I was not going to give these guys an inch. I would be on this course.

I was disappointed that Irena wasn't on the panel when I went in for my interview. It threw me off. I had opened up to her the day I'd come to the office and I thought her encouragement meant I would surely be successful. But sitting in front of two men and a woman, all looking at me very seriously and asking me questions about things I had already told their colleague, it felt off and wrong. These were *those* people – the kind who *took* things *from* you, not ones who brought things to you. I started to feel my defences go up, but I slowed my breathing, clutched my folder and decided to do my best.

'Your application, the essay you wrote, Katriona, was very enjoyable,' the woman said.

'Thank you for the interview,' I said. 'I'm a bit nervous.' In the theatre course we had learned to put words on our feelings, as people will relate better to you that way.

They asked me what I understood of the Trinity Access Programme and I lectured them on it. There wasn't a stone unturned by me that past week, and they found out stuff from me in that interview about the course that they didn't even know themselves.

'What would you like to do as a career?' they asked.

I told them I wanted to be an English teacher. I told them that teachers had been a huge support to me, and I wanted to do the same for others.

'Would you like to tell me what you're reading at the moment?' the taller of the two men, Ray, asked me. His eyes lit up and he leaned forward.

I was delighted to. I had been reading a great book, *The Road Less Travelled* by M. Scott Peck, and I had been completely intrigued by it. I told them as much.

'Tell me what you think the book is about?' the other man said. His name was also Ray.

I think I knew then that I had a place. Once I started talking about the book, the theories I had, the way the pages lifted and formed pictures in my head, the frustration of having nobody in my life to bounce these ideas off – of what it all meant – I saw it in their faces. I was in.

I'd got the letter in the morning and hung on to it for hours. I knew it was all over once I opened it, and despite my confidence after the interview, I had convinced myself it would be a rejection. That place wasn't for me. Of course not. All the dreaming I had been doing over the last few weeks, imagining myself writing essays and having opinions, that was all going to disappear. I knew it.

When I finally opened the letter, as I stood leaning against my kitchen counter, it took me ages to get to the bit saying I had a place. I couldn't see through the words for the message, I was so nervous.

We are delighted to offer you a place . . .

I burst into tears. It was my first real taste of 'making it' and it felt light, like gravity loosened a bit.

I rang my dad, the man who had turned down a place in Trinity all those years earlier. I could hear his breathing quicken, he took a little while to answer and I could tell he was in tears too.

'Can I have the letter? I want to frame it,' he said.

'But it's just the offer,' I said.

'It's the best news I have ever had,' he said. 'Your grandad would have been thrilled with you, so he would.'

That made me both happy and sad at the same time.

17

When I told people I knew that I was going to Trinity, I had one of a few reactions. Some people were excited, some were filled with pride. But most were worried.

'What about your book? Do you lose your rent allowance?' my friend Ashley said to me.

'No, I can keep my payments while I'm studying,' I said, 'for three years.'

'And then what?' She shook her head. 'Ah here, Katriona, come on, what will you do then?'

'I'll get a job!' I said. I faked incredulity, because deep down I was terrified. What if this was all a mistake, what if I didn't finish the course and lost my social welfare book? There was no way I could survive without it.

'What about the young lad?' she asked me. 'Who will mind him and all the bits he will need?'

John was in the second class in O'Connell's, down the road. It was within walking distance of our small basement flat on North Great Charles Street, just over from Mountjoy Square.

'Me!' I said, frowning at her. 'He comes first, Ashley, but . . . well . . . will you help me?'

She was delighted to. On the days when I was in college until five, Ashley would go to my flat and mind John. I gave her cash, the small allowance paid to me by Trinity for childcare.

The Trinity Access Programme ran – and still does – in Goldsmith Hall, a modern building at the back of Trinity on a corner bounded by Westland Row and Pearse Street. The building adjoins Pearse Station. So it is literally across the road from the main Trinity campus, the one with the beautiful old buildings that most people picture when they hear the word 'Trinity'. The course ran in two rooms, M48 and M35 – I have those numbers stamped into my brain. Because of their location you hardly needed to go into the main campus at all.

For the first two weeks of college we were able to get a flavour of different subjects: English, science, the arts and humanities. Once again I saw the impact of good teachers. My science professor was very charismatic, and I loved the class so much I almost took that as my subject. But his classes were on the main campus, not our usual building, and I hated walking over there. I felt so exposed among the 'real' students.

I had a chip on my shoulder. I thought the world consisted of people like me and people like *them*. There was no in-between. And for me it seemed like they had a familiar uniform – flowing skirts, tailoring, woollen jumpers. Their expensive unkemptness reminded me of the kids I'd served in the Institute. My uniform was jeans and tracksuits. If I could tell the difference between us on sight, I knew they could too. I saw the 'rich kids' as a group who oozed confidence and knew exactly what they were doing, and then there was us, the poor people, a group of us who moved around the college like a timid school of fish, unsure, nervous and not meant to be there.

The teachers for the two-week tasters were passionate people and champions of the access programme. The subjects were well introduced, and I knew which ones I favoured, but that didn't matter because I was going to choose my subjects based on the timetable. The most convenient schedule was the only way I could do this. People really don't understand but being a single mother is hair-raising, and it's not just about money – even with all the money in the world it would still be a battle against time. Children need to be brought to school, picked up, fed and cared for. Being a single mother is not conducive to the full-time focus that learning establishments need and expect from you.

I was committing to a full-time course of study without the ability to do it full-time. Childcare is expensive and I had no real support. I had to be home as much as I could be. The fewer early starts and late finishes the better. So I chose my subjects based on the contact hours. It didn't upset me to make my choices like that, being in college was enough. I just wanted to learn and so it didn't matter. I followed what worked – for me, it was enough to be there at all.

The classes I took were English, psychology, philosophy and law, alongside the compulsory classes in study skills, guidance and maths. I took higher level maths. I wasn't sure if I would need it at all, because I wasn't sure what I wanted to do, but I didn't want to shoot myself in the foot should I need it later.

Instantly, I knew English – surprisingly – was not for me. I love reading, I love the way the story plays out over the pages and images and emotions appear in my head, prompted by them. For me, reading is an escape. But in college I was being asked to reach past the emotions and images given to me by the author, past the window into the world that I could escape to, to find something they didn't necessarily want me to know. I was being asked to stretch every sentence out, to find reference points and meanings in everything.

I hated it. I didn't want to see things in books that ruined the story. I didn't want the truth; I wanted the fantasy. I wouldn't have been inspired to be strong even when I was scared, like the little girl in *The BFG*, if I'd known it was Dahl writing about himself and his daughters, in their safe middle-class cottage in England. If twelve-year-old me had known that Narnia was not in fact Narnia but a metaphor for heaven, lost to evil, it would have cut me out and set me aside, and I wouldn't have been side by side with the Pevensie children fighting for truth. The messages of those books go in, you live those stories; I didn't want to dissect them. I had few pleasures in my life – reading was one of them and I wouldn't give my books up.

But when it came to the other subjects, the new information was like food to my soul. In law I learned about intent, how you cannot commit the crime of murder unless you intend to kill. I learned about the humanities, about Aristotle, Plato. I learned about metaphysics and the principles of being, of identity and of space and time.

I spent my days thinking. Sitting in the class forming and sharing ideas, getting things wrong, hitting the mark. I knew who I was in those classes and what I had always been intended for. That question I had asked myself as I scrubbed the toilet floors in Connolly Station – *What am I here for?* – the answer was *this*. It's a cliché, but I found myself. I was on the beam.

Of course, I was dealing with constant reminders of what everyone else thought I was for. My mother was drinking, constantly drunk. My father was leaning on me to cope with her. I was carrying all of this baggage every day, weighed down by my life and buoyed up by the coursework. It should have been the other way round. I loved college, it meant everything to me, but no road is easy when you're being shot at from the sidelines. Sometimes you can't help but duck for cover.

I made it harder for myself, cracked open the chip on my shoulder and got inside it. Everyone seemed out to get me, everyone was trying to stop me – these were things I believed. I watched a group form on the access course, and I felt on the outside of it. Nothing they could say to try to bring me in felt real. 'Are you coming for coffee?' the girls would ask. I'd say no, feeling like they didn't want me there anyway, they were just asking to be polite. So after enough rejection the group forged on without me. And even though I refused invitations and didn't want to be around them, I felt left out.

The truth was, I didn't have the confidence to make friends. I judged myself too harshly and so believed others did too. And I suffered feelings of rejection because I needed social interactions to survive, as all humans do, I needed to belong. It always felt like they were all okay, and I was not. I was the odd one out, and so I dug the imaginary trench between us deeper.

Instead of a friendship group, during my first year at Trinity, I found myself pseudo-parents, an older man named Marius, who was from Romania, and a woman,

Liz, in her late fifties. Both of them coddled me in college, keeping track of me, helping me with comprehension, chatting to me in gentle ways. They showed me patience.

'You do the maths homework?' Marius always checked in with me on that subject. He knew I struggled.

'I just don't get it,' I said, and his hand went out for my book, pulling two chairs out. I was relieved; I knew he would help me, he always did.

'How do you know this stuff, Marius?' I said.

'I am an engineer back home,' he told me, 'but it's nothing to have a Romanian qualification here, so I have to repeat everything.'

'Ah, God,' I said, 'that sounds like a nightmare.'

'It is a nightmare,' he admitted as he opened the book and began to teach me.

I complained later to Liz.

'Maths is killing me,' I said.

She folded her arms and pursed her lips.

'Want to drop down?' she said. 'Do ordinary? So you don't fail?'

Fail? That was not me. I wouldn't be dropping down anything. I got on with it and passed.

TAP gave you tasters of everything and then set you up to do interviews for the degree courses. I really wanted to do psychology, so even though I was buoyed up by the offer of places in philosophy and in social studies, I was really unsure of the interview coming up for psychology. I knew I was going to Trinity either way, but I wanted what I wanted and the thought of failing – I just couldn't. It would have felt like I wasn't good enough.

I always thought I was going to get found out. Does that sound crazy? It's the best way to describe it. I felt as though I was an interloper.

In the interview for the psychology degree, I remember they asked me about my motivation. I knew I shouldn't say that I wanted to understand people better – we had been coached and warned not to make it personal – so I said I liked science. One of the interviewers asked me if Trinity was what I imagined academia to be like, sitting there with his tweed jacket, specs on the end of his nose and unruly grey hair that headed off on one side like a tree on a cliff.

'Yes,' I said truthfully.

'What theories do you enjoy?' the other interviewer asked. Oh, he was a maverick, corduroys and sunglasses on a chain.

'Freud,' I said and instantly wished I hadn't. I hated Freud.

'Oh yes?' he asked. 'What about Freud interests you?'

I couldn't think of one reason, so I babbled. 'Well, like, if you dreamed of towers, for example,' I could not believe the words coming out of my mouth, 'you know, the way they are standing up, like erect . . .' They nodded, and one of them grimaced, wishing perhaps he had never asked. 'I suppose,' I said, 'that's like you aren't able to process how you feel about . . . like –' I gulped – in for a penny in for a pound – 'willies.'

The air was dead. I was also dead. And so were they.

'Sorry,' I said.

One of them fumbled with papers; the other one noticed something very interesting out of the window. But I got the place.

It was tough at that point because there were more access students than places available. So even though we were all together in this group, we were also in competition with each other. My friend Liz didn't get into the course she wanted, psychology, and I did. When I saw my name on that list, I let out a whoop of joy. And then I turned round and saw her crumble. That was hard.

18

My friend Lindsey was staying with me. She had spent too long in a bad relationship, she was trying to recover from heroin addiction and her boyfriend, an addict called Danny, was pulling her back under. So she left him. He didn't take that news well. He had locked her in the flat for days and abused her badly. By the time she came to my place she was bruised and battered, with bloodstained clothes and a swollen lip. She was terrified and so was I.

'We should get Derek down,' I said, 'just in case Danny comes here.'

She agreed. We knew the door of my flat wouldn't hold against an angry man. We were in real danger. So I called Derek and he came down. And out of boredom he made a pass. I had no self-esteem, I didn't refuse it and we slept together. Within three weeks I knew I was pregnant.

When that happened, there are no words to describe the shame and panic. I knew there was no way I could have another baby. John was finally at an age when things were easier, he was thriving in his football club, and I was thriving in the access programme. The gold under my feet would turn to stone again. I just knew it.

My friend Laura came over.

'I can't have another baby on my own,' I said, 'everything's just starting . . .' and she held my hand.

She said nothing, she just let me decide what I had to do. She didn't play devil's advocate or tell me what I needed. Just gave her full support. No judgement or pressure. It's what all women should have: unconditional trust.

I called my dad, and I asked him for a lend of four hundred euro.

'I haven't got my cheque from Trinity yet,' I lied.

'What cheque?' he asked.

'Oh, there's a cheque for books we get but I need them now, Dad, any chance?'

He said okay. I felt the relief down to my toes.

Derek had ignored every text I'd sent him, but he answered the one looking for money for an abortion. He arrived within the day to give me the cash. Then he went and told everyone.

Some people pretended they hadn't heard, but I could see they had by the looks they gave me. Other people asked me straight out, 'Have you got that sorted yet?' as if I was dragging my heels. I was mortified that I was pregnant for Derek. After he gave me the money I never saw him again.

Laura said she would come with me. It was only for the day – we would fly into Liverpool at half six a.m. and fly back at nine p.m. But I couldn't get an appointment in the UK for four weeks, so I had to wait.

Being pregnant when you don't want to be feels like a death sentence. Living with a pregnancy you can't keep is a stress that is deep and fierce. There is no relief from it. I can only describe the wait as surreal. I was not Katriona O'Sullivan, I was something else, something that looked like her and sat in class in college pretending to be her, but for those weeks I was something else. I was not my son's mother, just a copy of her, my kisses held nothing of my heart. For that time, I was just waiting, waiting. I wanted to reverse, go back. I wanted the world to spin faster, to get to the day and get my soul back.

When the time arrived, I went to the airport with Laura. I brought nothing with me, just a nightie and slippers and some pads. The flight to Liverpool had other girls on it. You could see it in their faces. I knew them by the expression in their eyes – it was like looking into a mirror.

We took the train to the clinic; on the Dublin side we had been given maps and instructions, and Laura took charge of following them. The clinic looked like any office above a shop. Unassuming and clean. The walls were lined with waiting girls and their partners.

I had my bloods taken when I arrived and then I sat with them, waiting.

'Katriona O'Sullivan?' The nurse called my name and I jumped up and crossed the floor to her cubicle as fast as I could.

'Katriona,' she said with this look on her face.

I was alarmed by it.

'Did you ever have a blood transfusion?' she asked me.

I nodded. 'Yeah, I did have one before,' I said, thinking of John's birth.

'You have an antibody in your blood, Katriona,' she said softly.

I nodded. *So?*

'We can't do the procedure today,' she said.

Please.

She shook her head. 'We can't do the procedure, you must come back tomorrow – we will have the product you need tomorrow,' she said.

'I have to go back to Ireland tonight,' I said. My ribcage felt like it was crushing my heart. I couldn't swallow. My throat was closing.

Please.

She understood. She held my hand. She shook her head.

'We cannot do the procedure without the product you need, Katriona. You have to come back tomorrow. Here is your appointment.' She handed me a card.

I left the cubicle and started towards the door. Laura

followed me out and down the stairs and outside, where I walked up the road to get away from the place. She caught up with me after a bit. 'Katriona, what's wrong?'

I burst into tears. 'They can't do it till tomorrow,' I said.

She just stood there, looking at me and back to the clinic, as I told her the story.

'Jesus, Katriona,' she said. 'I can't stay . . . I . . .'

I nodded, assured her that was okay. And it was. I was an animal in a trap; I wanted to be by myself, so I could gnaw this pain away alone.

'Where will you stay?' she asked.

'They gave me the name of a bed and breakfast,' I said.

'How much is it?' she said. 'Jesus, Katriona, I haven't a penny.'

'I have to ring my dad,' I said, and felt my chest tightening with anxiety. We went to a phone box. I rang my dad and told him where I was and what I was there for. I explained the procedure, the transfusion, the need for an overnight stay. He said nothing.

'I need you to call this bed and breakfast and book me in, Dad, and then book me a flight for tomorrow night home,' I said.

'Right,' he said. I could feel the disapproval in the way he clipped his words. I gave him the number.

'I'll call you back in half an hour, Dad,' I said and hung up.

I insisted Laura leave me at that point. I couldn't speak, I just wanted to stare into space. We went to the train and I walked away as soon as she said goodbye. In my young life I had built this perception of my dad and of who I was to him, which was one of a caring, loving father and a good daughter. I was his favourite. My mum had Michael and my dad had me. It was simply the way things were in our family and everyone knew it. So when that was shaken, when my dad was off with me, it felt, in a way, like someone had cut the tie to my anchor and I was adrift alone. It made everything seem worse. Everything darker.

I called my dad back and he told me he had booked everything, so I walked down to the bed and breakfast where the woman there patted me on the arm and gave me a fresh towel and key and offered me a cup of tea that I said no to.

The room was small, with cream walls and an industrial carpet in some sort of red. There was a single bed along the wall and a small table. A cell.

I sat on the bed. I looked at the wall. The hours went by. I tried to sleep but it was pointless. When the hours were up, I dressed and walked to the clinic. Children and their mothers passed me on their way to school; a man swept the street outside his house with a cheery whistle.

Then I was there, in the clinic, and I was being taken care of. Nurses were telling me not to worry, everything would be sorted out. My eyes felt bare and sore in their sockets. They put a needle in my arm and knocked me out. When I woke up a nurse was chucking my cheek and saying my name. She shook my knee.

'Katriona, pet, wake up now,' she said. She walked around the other side of the bed, unhooked the side of it and swung it down.

'Is it done?' I said. I grabbed her arm. 'Is it done?'

She nodded and said, 'Yes, yes, it's done.'

My heart beat. *Boom.*

I burst into tears.

'Thank you very much,' I said over and over again.

The nurse gave me a cuddle and I cried on her shoulder, and it was not regret, it was pure relief. I had been given a reprieve.

I do not regret having a termination.

I regret the childhood I had that taught me I was worthless.

I regret that when my dad picked me up at the airport he acted disgusted with me and whenever my mother had a few drinks she would throw it in my face.

I regret existing in a culture that treats women who need help like criminals.

I regret that I couldn't have a termination in Ireland then. By having to involve people – Derek, my dad – and them telling other people – my friends and neighbours, my mother – I had a pressure I would never have had if proper healthcare had been available to me.

I was relieved and had made the best choice for me, but I was under a different pressure now. I had this trauma of shame. I had been stoned in the public square and I needed to heal.

Before I got pregnant, I was starting to do well in college. I was doing so well I was offered places on three degree courses, conditional on my exam results: philosophy, psychology and social studies. Yet, the better I did, the more I wanted to give up. My family were being crazy, my dad was ringing me fifty times a day to discuss my mother, who was drunk all the time. College had always been a juggling act but now I had to focus so hard to keep that ball in the air, the others started to drop, and they were knocking me off balance.

I wanted to do a psychology degree, I really did. Irena told me I'd have to get my head down, get my exams and work hard. I *was* working hard. My head *was* down. I had been living so cleanly, cooking good food at home, never drinking alcohol. There wasn't much more I could give here. *These people have no idea*, I thought to myself.

After the termination, I started to turn on myself again. I started letting go of college work, dragging my heels, leaving questions I knew the answers to hanging in the air in class. I wasn't present. I was distracted, I'd lost self-belief, had no reason to be there. Everything they said about me was true.

Pissy pants. Smelly. Dirty trash. Thick bitch. Mouth. Gymslip mum. Sponger. Waster. Common. Slut. Slapper. Stupid. Stupid. Stupid. Stupid.

And so, a week before my exams, with the passion of a woman about to self-sabotage, I dressed myself up to the nines, dropped my son to my dad's, rang my friends and went out. I told myself I deserved the break, needed to let loose, just once. I'd been working so hard. I needed the stress relief that a night out would bring. I went to a party on Talbot Street, someone offered me a glass of champagne, and I took it without so much as a flinch. I didn't go home for five days.

You see, it is hard to swim against a current. It's easier to go with the flow. If you have lived in stress and disharmony all your life, that is the current you tend to go with, even if it will end with you in deeper water. In psychology we call this a set point; it is where we are most comfortable. Once we establish the norm, we are driven to maintain that level, to stay within our normal range. My set point at that time was stressed and afraid: I'd lived most of my life that way. So when I returned to self-destruction, I was simply lifting my feet and going with the flow. In a way, I was taking a break from pushing through. I was more comfortable with fear and failure. When I was at my lowest, that was what I looked for.

Someone banging on your door before nine is never good. I contemplated ignoring it, but it was likely to be my mum, so I went out and answered it. It was Irena.

'What's going on?' she said.

I wanted to shut the door. I'd spent a week at my parents', rebellious and defiant. My dad had found me at five a.m. in the Blue Lion surrounded by strangers, out of my head. He had dragged me home to his house and sobered me up.

Trinity was not for me; I had decided this. I didn't want to go any more, and everyone needed to get off my back. Now this middle-class busybody Trinity head was at my door? This was stepping over the line. I was a grown woman. I could decide for myself what I would or would not be doing.

Just fuck off.

'What's going on?' she asked me again.

'You're wasting your breath, Irena,' I said. 'I'm not able for it, I'm not doing it.'

'Not doing your exams?' She looked so surprised. 'Katriona, you've worked a whole year for this, they are three days away, come on . . . of course you're doing the exams.'

'Thanks for everything, Irena,' I said, and I meant it, 'but I'm not coming back.'

She half laughed when I said that, but she spoke very seriously. 'If I have to come over here and drag you by the scruff over to do those exams, then fine, I will,' she said. 'YOU are not dropping out.'

'I can't do it,' I said. 'I can't manage.'

'You have managed,' she said. 'Give yourself some credit.'

That was a good point. She saw through me. She saw, somehow, that my comfort zone, my set point, was in a world of chaos and disarray. Being focused, and looking to my future, was uncomfortable and alien. It felt wrong. Especially when around me everyone else resisted.

I was someone who thrived on praise, I was hugely rewarded by it. I flourish with authoritative people and Irena had a knack with me. Up until that point I'd wanted to please her and worked hard to do so. I am sure that without the drive to please this woman, I might not have done so well. I never left college work till last, I always handed in to a deadline, always turned up.

So, imagine what happened to me when I was facing the opposite of praise. Until she turned up on my doorstep I couldn't have gone back to college of my own accord because the thought of being in Irena's bad books made me feel awful. I thought I had already blown it.

'Katriona,' she said, 'the time to drop out, to let it all go, is *after* the exams, not a week before them.'

'I –'

'No excuses, no answers,' she said, waving a finger. 'See you early Friday.'

She walked away, I shut the door and burst out crying. I headed straight out the door once I was sure she was gone and walked over to the Five Lamps, to the office where Joe was. On the way I talked to myself, told myself these people hadn't a clue about me. What would they know? They acted like it was easy, but it wasn't easy. I didn't have what it took to do these exams. I wasn't the kind of person to go to college anyway. Why was I pretending I was?

This Trinity journey I was on, I told myself, it was just a way for me to escape the trauma of the year before. The way I'd been treated by men, especially that one man, the way it had all played out and I'd got so burned. That was what this college crap was really about.

What I wanted, what Katriona O'Sullivan wanted, was a council house, my book, a cash-in-hand part-time job and a man to bring another wage home. My son would be happy and have what he needed. I wouldn't be getting above my station. Trinity was a waste of time and energy. I wasn't going back. I was my own woman. The answer was no.

As I came in the door, Joe was halfway through

smoking a cigarette. He looked up and said, 'Oh jayz, what now?' But it was kindly, warm. I couldn't even start the story, but he knew from the state of me I had fallen out of sobriety.

'They don't understand in Trinity, Joe,' I said. 'They don't know what it's like.'

'If they knew what it was like,' he said, 'what could they change?'

I thought about it. 'They could be a bit easier on people.'

'Well, you'd still have to do your exams either way,' he said. 'And maybe you need the hard push this time, because your woman is right, you have to do them exams.'

I don't know what I wanted to hear but it wasn't that.

'The time to drop out is after the exams, Katriona,' Joe said. 'Commitment can't be half-hearted.'

I left his office and went home. I got my books out, spread them on my kitchen table and started to cram.

19

Passing the exams at the end of the access year was a push to get back on track and keep going. I stopped drinking. I went to see my counsellor every week and I was going nowhere near men. I mean nowhere near them. I never wanted to feel that level of shame again.

'And you're starting college again soon?' Marian asked me one day.

'Yes!' I said. I had just got myself some new notebooks and pens and a lovely bag. This was going to be the best thing, I told myself. I was nervous, terrified even, because people kept saying the workload was totally different, and I knew there would be no coddling in the mainstream. I knew I had almost blown everything at the end of the access course, but there were reasons . . . I allowed myself the glitch. This year I was staying away from everything and everyone, getting my head down into studying and being a good mother for my son.

When I went in the first day, I went through Front Gate, the main entrance to the campus on College Green. The hall for our intake session was huge. I saw the mature students sitting up the front, the retired people with their brand-new computers and ready fingers and the middle-aged looking for a career switch. I didn't belong with them. At the back were the school leavers. I didn't belong with them either.

I sat in the middle and kept my eyes down. I wasn't here for friendships; I was here for me. Then, 'Oh my God, wait! It's you, isn't it?'

I looked up. A girl around eighteen years old, blonde dreadlocks and a nose piercing in both nostrils. She had bright green eyeliner and a wide smile. She was speaking to me.

Shit.

I recognized this girl. She was one of the kids in the Institute I had served sausage rolls and cans of Coke to a couple of years before. I'd play this by ear. I looked at her blankly.

'I don't know who "you" is,' I said, with no tone in my voice. I lifted my chin.

'You were my dinner lady!! It's you, isn't it?' She used her 'outside voice' but we were inside, in a room with great acoustics. I blew out my cheeks and gave a pathetic smile.

'Yep,' I said.

This one was harmless, but I was embarrassed.

'But what are you doing here?' she said. She wasn't being mean. Just silly.

'Ah, come on,' I said. 'Did you not know dinner ladies have brains?'

She stared innocently back at me, gently shaking her head with the look of a child that's seen a fairy.

'Well, that's amazing,' she said, and my patience ran a little thin. 'Fair dues to you,' she added.

Fair dues? *Feck off.* These people had no idea.

'There's another guy in this course from my class,' she said as if I would be glad at the reunion.

I just nodded my way out of the conversation and avoided her after that.

I'm not going to tell you stories about the interactions of college life, about the guy who didn't pull his weight in the group tasks but got the marks anyway. I'm not going to tell you about the trips to the shop during lunch or lying in Stephen's Green with my books wishing I could just bloody eat them and absorb the information that way. We all have those college stories. I'm not going to repeat them. But I will tell you about *me* and *my life* and how it went during my college years.

I made my way through Trinity out of a sense of accomplishment that became addictive. I wanted the feeling of knowledge, the full brain exhaustion that classes gave me. Perhaps it was something I picked up being a girl among boys, but I wanted to be the best one, just as good as them, and that became an internal competitiveness that pushed me forward.

As a kid I learned to outsmart other people. It was how I survived. I watched and listened to the small things, picking up what I needed to get through. I eavesdropped on my mother's phone calls, read my father's letters, looked through their pockets. What information did I need to make my situation better?

I could also read the smallest changes in people's energy. The children of addicts are often gifted with this superpower, intuitively knowing when the mood has changed. A dip in good humour could easily become anger if not monitored and managed with favours.

Strangely, that stood to me in Trinity. When my lecturers mentioned that something would come up, or could come in exams, I studied that thing until I knew it backwards. I watched my lecturers' responses to other students and figured out what the correct answer was faster than others, so I focused on the right things.

'Can any of you offer an example of a risk factor of childhood?' the lecturer asked us in a small tutorial group.

The girl beside me shifted in her seat. There was a folded jacket and a good leather book bag on the floor beside her. Her boots were new, clean white socks peeping over them. As she scribbled notes, her fingers were smooth and white around a black pen. I looked at my own fingers where the stains of my fake tan had gathered in the creases. I pulled my sleeves down.

The tutor picked on her. 'Sadhbh? Can you give me one example of a risk factor?'

Sadhbh frowned. My head buzzed with them, issues I had faced as a kid – the list was so long.

She said, 'I don't think there are any?'

Her response knocked me for six. I stared at her. I wondered what it would be like to have the idea that childhood was a safe place. Because mine was nowhere near it.

It was those things that kept me from interacting fully with my classmates. In my own area, in Audrey's kitchen, or standing chatting outside the school with my friend Ashley, or even on the Community Employment schemes or vocational training courses, I was one of the group. Because everyone had a reason to be there, all were unemployed or struggling single parents.

But here in Trinity, I couldn't readily get a fix on other students. So I erred on the side of caution, presuming that everyone was a 'Sadhbh'. They hadn't been around people like me, and they wouldn't understand me. They were floating in pools and I was drowning out at sea.

I kept myself to myself. When they chatted to me I chatted back, but always, just as it threatened to go past small talk, I ended the conversation and left the room. I used to go to talk to the staff – not the lecturers, but the security staff, the catering staff, the receptionists and maintenance workers. I knew them all by name and always stopped to chat; finding a friendly face, I felt recognized and understood.

The energy in my world was one that was full of conflict, and so I was comfortable with that. I preferred the idea of someone raising hell with me than keeping it to themselves. I didn't like politeness, it unnerved me. I second-guessed myself too much.

The discomfort I felt was partially down to the ideology I had built up around who had the 'right' to go to Trinity. I felt like a charity case.

I used to spend time in one of the two bars in Trinity, the Buttery. It's a busy place and I would hole up in the corner with my bags and books between lectures. I felt at home there, I got to know the staff, and found friends behind the counters. I told myself these were my people, I could – or maybe should – be behind the counter and not out here reading psychology. You could smoke inside then and asking for a lighter was a great way of getting a chat going with one of my own. The service workers, the working classes. I felt at home around them. I knew where I was.

After everything was dealt with in Liverpool and I was flying home, I had come to a resolution. I had decided – and I knew I was serious – to stay away from men. I was not available, and that was on my terms.

I was good at that. I had always been good at keeping to these kinds of decisions – rock bottom has that effect. I focused on college. I wanted to do well and I wanted the praise that came with top marks. It hardened my bones.

But at Christmas I failed statistics. The results were always pinned on these huge wooden boards, the first-year board, the second-year board, etc. I looked for my student number and realized I'd failed, and I just wanted to run out of Trinity and never come back.

See? You're an imposter.

Hey, stupid, yeah you. Get out of here.

I didn't want – not in the moment – to know why I'd failed or to make any calm or good judgement calls on that situation. I wanted to drop it and drop out. Thankfully the TAP offices were open, and I headed there.

'Ah,' said Irena when I told her. I hadn't got half the sentence out before I broke into a sob.

'I can't do it,' I said. 'It's not for me.'

'It's one exam, Katriona,' she said and the secretary behind her, who was holding a cup of tea, nodded and said, 'Everybody fails one, it's a learning curve.'

I stopped crying. 'What can I possibly learn from failing?'

She put her cup down. 'What you need to focus your efforts on.'

From then on, I gave statistics more time than other subjects.

Things started to change after that, in the way I used my time. I'd been studying what I loved and avoiding what I didn't. Now I studied more of what I didn't like and didn't get.

The year went by, and it was Valentine's Day. I met a girl I knew, Suzanne, to walk to the AA meeting in South William Street. I was so good and clean and sober and focused. I really felt like my mind was my own, I had energy and patience. I loved my course. I was, as Audrey liked to say, on the beam.

The place was full when we got there so we sat in a row close to the back. I looked across and saw my friend Mark. I waved. He leaned back and waved at me and I noticed he was with that guy Dave who had shared the house with Derek. I hadn't seen Derek again and the sight of his housemate shook me a little. I looked away, down at the ground. I felt judged and humiliated. I hated that he knew for sure.

I tried to escape after the meeting was over, but Mark caught me before I could. I played it breezy.

'Ah, hiya, Mark,' I said.

He looked over at Suzanne, who was sorting through her bag, putting the handouts from the meeting into the side pocket, putting on her coat and fixing the hood of it under her hair.

'Didn't know you were friends with Suzanne?' he said.

'Ah, we just walked down together,' I said. 'I don't know her well, but she's a nice girl.'

'I know,' he said and looked over again.

I looked too. Ah. The penny dropped.

'Why don't yous come up for coffee?' he said as she came over.

Suzanne's eyes lit up. 'Ah, hiya, Mark,' she said.

'Come up,' he said to me. 'My old friend Dave is coming too, he's sound.'

'It's Valentine's Day,' I said, 'sure there'll be a queue at my door.' I winked.

'Ah do, come up,' he said.

I looked at Suzanne and she nodded and said, 'Why not?'

We waited outside by the railings for Dave, who had been chatting to someone else.

'Hiya,' he said to me, not quite catching my eye.

I felt the shame again. *Tramp.*

Brush it off.

I raised my chin. 'Course we will come for coffee,' I said. 'Let me just lock my moped.'

We walked back to Mark's place and went in.

'So, girls, any Valentine cards?' Mark said.

'Oh yeah, millions,' Suzanne said.

'I got roses, chocolates and a bottle of Blue Jeans perfume!' I said.

'No way, did you?' Suzanne thought I was serious.

I shook my head. 'Who would be giving me anything,

are you mad?' I said with a loud laugh, as if the idea was ludicrous.

'Ah, sorry,' she said. 'I love that perfume.'

'I used to have one of the big bottles of it,' I said, 'it's lovely.'

'What do you wear now?' Dave suddenly said.

'I can't afford perfume,' I said, and I was embarrassed. I wished I'd lied.

There was an exchange of glances between the two men, and they went into the small galley kitchen off the sitting room where myself and Suzanne were sitting together on the couch. We heard hurried whispers. Some sort of plan was being concocted.

Dave came back out. 'Eh, Katriona, do you want to come down to get chips with me?'

Mark appeared, looking nonchalant.

I looked at Suzanne, raised my eyebrows.

'Oh, I'd love chips,' she said.

I stood up. 'Grand, okay,' I said and followed Dave down to the car.

'Love the car,' I said, appraising it as he unlocked it, sat in the driver's seat and moved a jacket off the front seat for me to get in. It was clean inside and there was an air freshener in the grille, orange scent. Men like Dave, the ones with good jobs and focus, always had nice cars. I didn't know many men like that.

'Thanks,' he said. The drive to the chipper was short,

and he pulled in outside, hopped out and ran in. I saw him order and then he came back.

'Ten minutes,' he said.

I nodded slowly; this was going to be awkward. Suzanne really owed me one.

Dave cleared his throat. 'I always wanted to say to you – about Derek,' he said.

My defences engaged.

'What?' I said, ready to exit the car and walk home. It wasn't far.

'I couldn't believe a girl like you would be with someone like him,' he said.

I was so shocked I stared at him. Out of me and Derek, he thought I was the better one? Dave was so clean and tanned, with such bright blue eyes. I liked his face so much when I took the time to look at it.

'A girl like me?' I asked.

'Yeah, a girl like you,' he said and hopped out of the car to retrieve the chips that were on the counter waiting. Only then did I think of saying I couldn't believe a nice fella like him would be living in a house with a low-life like Derek.

When he got back into the car, I had caught my breath. A man speaking to me so straight and telling me in no uncertain terms that he thought I was *something*. Well, it knocked me for six. I felt like a million dollars sitting there in my tracksuit.

The car felt like a cocoon in the dark as we drove back. For once, I was struck dumb.

'I'll just nip in for smokes,' Dave said, pulling into the shop sharply. As I sat there, I thought about his face, and how I'd never noticed how handsome he was before. I'd just seen a good clean-living man and so ignored him. I wasn't in that race.

When we got back to the house Mark had already made coffee and the two men served us chips and coffee; on our plates were two cards, one each, for Valentine's Day.

Later, Dave dropped me to my moped.

'Can I borrow your jacket?' I said. 'It was warm earlier but it's freezing now.' It was an excuse, I wanted to give him a reason to call me. If he didn't want to, he could ask Mark to get it. It was a safe bet. He handed it over, made a joke. I said goodbye and started my bike. I didn't look back.

The next few days were okay. I thought about Dave, but I told myself this was residual fear of rejection. I calmed myself, talked myself out of my old ways when I wanted to casually stroll by Mark's to see if I could spot Dave's car or accidentally text him. Men had never treated me well, so I was going to treat myself well. This was a new start.

It still didn't stop my heart from pounding when Dave did text. It didn't stop a smile spreading across my face and a flutter coursing through my stomach.

Can I grab my jacket some time? the text read.

Yeah no problem. But knock after my little boy is in bed.

When he called round, I asked him if he wanted tea and he said yes and sat in my kitchen drinking and smoking cigarettes until the early hours. Dave on one end of my small kitchen table, me on the other end. He told me all about his mam and showed kindness when he did. He talked about his job, and he made jokes that I laughed out loud to.

It must have been two a.m. when he realized he had smoked all my cigarettes and so he went out to replace them, even though I insisted it was fine.

'No way am I leaving you without smokes for the morning,' he said.

'Let me give you money,' I said when he came back with them, having run across to the garage.

He pushed my purse away, 'No way, don't be mad,' and then he said night and left. I stood at the door until he got into his car and then I closed it and leaned against the back of it for a moment. I really had a strong sense that *this* man, this man was my man.

Dave started dropping in for tea and texting me a little bit. Nothing too intense. I felt frustration but talked myself out of it. I begged myself to leave the ball in his court. Just let things happen. I wanted, as Marian said, to step out of my own way.

Eventually after weeks of patience, while I was

making a fifth cup of tea, Dave stood up from the table and approached me and said, 'Is this –' he made an inclusive gesture between us – 'just friends?'

Oh, thank God.

'I've enough friends, Dave,' I said, and he kissed me right away.

'Want to go for dinner with me?' he asked me as he left a little later.

'Yeah,' I said.

When he arrived the next night he had a bottle of Blue Jeans for me. I swear I would have married him there and then.

Getting involved wasn't a distraction, it was almost like a reason to persevere. I was attending college and doing my work as best I could, and things went from strength to strength with this great guy. And I wanted more of that, I wanted all of the dream.

So when I got my grant cheque, to cover my outlays for books and whatnot in retrospect, I went straight to a phone box and called him. 'Can you get off work next week?' I said without even saying hello.

'Yeah, think so,' he replied. 'Why?'

'I'm booking both of us to the Canaries.' It was the Easter break and I should have been studying but I talked myself into the idea that I needed this. I'd catch up. And the dream I'd had over the years, when I'd been lonely and upset, neglected and hurt, of someone I loved, who loved me too, that dream was coming true. But it felt too good for me.

We were sitting in a Spanish bar a week later, with two glasses of cola since neither of us drank, and I noticed Dave staring at a girl who was crossing the floor.

'Do you want me to get her number for you?' I asked him, then stood up, shoving the table. Dave steadied the glasses.

'Wait,' he said as I marched off.

My blood was boiling. There it was. He was just like all the rest. I was a fool.

'Come here,' he said, catching my arm just before we got to the room, 'I think I know her from Blanch, that's all.'

'Go and ask her, then,' I said, and twisted my arm out of his grip. This was it. I wanted to get it over and done with. He could dump me now. Just do it.

Just do it.

He grabbed my arm again, turned me back round.

'Don't you know how I feel –' he said, and the words caught in his throat. 'Katriona, I love you.'

'Oh yeah?' The anger dissipated; those words, I felt them fill me with strength. 'Well, I love you too.'

In second year, comfortable in this secure relationship, with my nine-year-old doing well in school and excelling at football, we moved out of Dublin city centre and decided to have another baby. Perhaps subconsciously I needed to heal the trauma of the termination, but the experience of being loved was empowering, and being a family seemed like second nature to both of us. I called him at work.

'Hey, Dave, I'm pregnant.'

'Pregnant?' He started to laugh. 'Ah, Katriona, are you serious? That's brilliant.'

I flashbacked to that cold call I had made to my child's father years before when he told me he was tired and to the one I'd made the year before to Derek when he hung up as soon as I spoke. The shame and fear were gone, replaced with confidence and excitement. It warmed my broken heart, put in another stitch.

I had the baby, Seán, in 2005. I studied on with a new baby. I didn't take any leave; I changed his nappy on my knee while reading through my notes and fed him into the night as I studied. I sat my second-year exams when he was three months old. I knew what I was doing by now, I knew how to study.

I know that, for me, college while pregnant and with a new baby should have been a struggle, but it didn't feel like it. I'd had a childhood filled with stress, it was my centre point, I was comfortable in it. Balancing everything, keeping it all going, that felt normal to me.

In third year, having to do a research project, I worked harder than I had ever worked in my life. I discovered that my childhood obsession with keeping tabs on my parents, my investigations and putting two and two together, had left me with the ability to research and join dots really well. I took on a topic that I could get my teeth into: looking at the difference between smokers, ex and current, in performing unconscious tasks. At the time the government was introducing warnings on packets of cigarettes. I was interested in finding out if the stimuli that is present in smokers was still present in ex-smokers, making them susceptible to relapse. It was a great project, and so I was confident that I would pass my degree, but I didn't want to skate along for a pass. It was important to me to do as well as I could. What was the point if I didn't? It would have been for nothing.

'The results are out in June, and if you guys are thinking about using this degree for anything decent in the future, a 2:1 is your only hope, okay?' our teachers repeated, over and over. I knew I had to do it.

The day the results were posted, I was absolutely terrified. Students were everywhere in Trinity that day, some with big red eyes, others elated. I went down to where the noticeboard was, where the results were posted. The A4 sheets pinned to it were so flimsy for the weight of what was on them. I heard the hisses of a few whispered curses and upset exclamations.

My throat tightened. An anxiety response.

What if I'd failed . . .

I jostled my way between the other students. I was face to face with the board. The sheet ran in order of grades; where other students ran their fingers down to find theirs, I ran my finger up from the bottom. It was unintentional, but I think about that a lot.

I didn't fail. I went past the 2:2s and into the short list of 2:1s. My number wasn't there. I ran my finger back down halfway before I looked up. My number was at the top. A loud 'Fucking yes!' escaped me. I clasped my hand over my mouth and then let it drop. I am who I am.

'*Fucking YESSSS!!*'

A first.

20

My dad was fifty-five when he was diagnosed with cancer. He was given a good chance to survive it, a really good one. He declined. I think I know why, now. He was the head of our family. The tsunami of chaos started with him, he was at the crest of the wave. And so none of us really believed he would actually die, least of all himself.

So much so that I declined Christmas with them that year. My mum was drinking heavily and causing trouble. Nothing new there. Christmas was always a disaster. My dad never gave you presents you would like; he gave you presents he wanted you to like. He always missed the mark. He would buy me tartan and cashmere when I wanted velour and fluff; he bought my mother pearls when she loved hoops. My dad was middle class, he was raised right, but we were not. Maybe he bought presents for who he thought we would have been had he taken a different road, not who we *were*. Either way, it hurt. It felt like we weren't good enough. I had my own family now and wanted to make it about my children instead of acting as a weird combination of babysitter and referee for my parents.

The following summer he died from throat cancer. He was sober, had been for years; at the end of it all he was just addicted to Solpadeine, and of course the smokes, sixty a day. He used to buy boxes of cheap Bensons from a woman he knew in Summerhill. They tasted like metal.

My life was blossoming by this time: I was reaching the end of my PhD, Dave and I had welcomed a third child, Tadhg, and got married. My children were happy and healthy, John now playing football professionally. My home life was calm. But my dad, twice a week, would keep me well connected to the chaos that came with being an O'Sullivan. My mum was drinking, there was drama in the family, there was always something.

I went to hospital appointments with him. It had always been that way as my mum was usually drunk. By now they were living in Galway. After my grandfather died, my father had sold the house in Clontarf and he and my mum had moved to Donabate. After a few years there, they moved to Ballinasloe, Co. Galway. Another fresh start, downsizing for the income. So he was doing his radiation treatment in Galway.

His body took it well. I used to go down there sometimes and stay over with him during his treatment in the hospice in Ballinasloe. The nurses loved him. Everybody loved Tony. He had charisma, even then.

I remember lying in the dark during his treatment, with streetlight coming in the window and skirting across the tiled floor, in a single bed facing my dad on another. He wasn't asleep so I wasn't either. I looked at him and he looked at me, in the dark.

'You and me, we're all clear now, aren't we?' he said. His voice was low and upset.

I just looked at him for that moment.

'I've made it up to you, haven't I?' he said. 'There's no bad between us?'

I could have told him. I could have listed off the agony I still felt day in day out over the childhood I'd had. I could have . . .

'Don't be silly, Dad,' I said, 'there is nothing bad between you and me, you're my hero.'

He slept then. And I lay in the dark and watched his chest rise and fall until the morning.

Months later, after he died, I was in my office in Trinity and I moved something and an envelope slid from under it on to the floor. It said 'Katriona' on it. It was my dad's handwriting. I remembered, it was a thesis I had asked him to proofread for me and forgotten about. There would be nothing in it for me now. But I opened it anyway.

A note.

I'm so proud of your achievements and your intellectual perusals, I'm here watching Avatar while your mum lives in chaos, I love you my Katriona, Dad.

After that episode, Tony got the all-clear following radiation and his life went back to normal. He had been right: he wasn't going to die. He called me twice a week, gave me the latest chaotic spin on the family. And I continued with my PhD studies.

This intense focus I had, getting to PhD, was becoming something else, a crusade perhaps. The skills of thinking were changing my brain, and I could almost literally feel the synapses of my mind expanding and making connections.

And I was waking up. I watched people who were born with silver spoons in their mouths talk about the 'right' of people like me to go to college. I listened to arguments about how college might not be 'a fit for everyone', even discussions of people's 'place' in society. I was getting angry.

In spring 2011 I got a call from my dad and he was slurring a little, using the wrong words. My mum said he was fine, just a kidney infection. But I knew, so I got into the car and drove down.

'I want vodka,' was the first thing he said to me. He was delusional, poisoned by toxins in his body that couldn't clear themselves. His organs were shutting down.

'Do you?' I said.

He shook his head, 'No.'

They put him in the high-dependency unit, cleared his blood. He felt better.

His neck was in a bad way, and I didn't need anyone to tell me that the cancer was back – I could see it – but I demanded to speak to someone anyway. I sat beside my dad when the doctor came in.

'Will he survive this?' I said.

The doctor looked at Tony.

'Doctor, will he survive this?' I asked again. I needed to know.

'That's not for you to ask,' the doctor said, 'that's for Tony to ask.'

I needed to know. I turned to my dad; his hands were grasping his knees. 'Dad, ask him, ask him.'

'Will I survive?' my dad asked, though I knew he didn't really want to know. But I did. *I needed to know.*

'No,' the doctor said, 'no, you won't survive.'

My mum stood up and left the room. My father's hands fell away from his knees and he nodded to himself, over and over. I saw his hands start to shake.

I shouldn't have insisted. At that moment I almost wished I hadn't. But *I* needed to know.

'How long?' my dad said.

'Less than a year,' the doctor said.

A week later I was standing in my office in Trinity when my phone rang.

'Katriona,' my dad said, 'can you come down?'

'Dad, I'm in work, what's wrong?'

'Katriona, can you come? I'm going to die, I'm going to die today,' he said.

I remember flinching with annoyance, overcome with this feeling that it was impossible, but . . . there was something in his voice. I hung up and called the ward. The nurse said my dad was fine. I took her word, and I went back to what I had been doing.

Then, not long later, the hospital rang me back and said that things had taken a sudden downturn and I should come after all.

Dave drove me down. We were there in hours.

The way my father died, he couldn't breathe. The cancer in his neck started to bleed and it was choking him. That was the worst thing. He had been terrified of that from the start. I couldn't understand why they had not given him morphine. They answered that they hadn't been sure since he was in recovery from addiction. That made me so angry – for God's sake, *please*, what was the harm now?

There was nothing peaceful for my dad at the end, there was no gentle exit from the world. He begged me for a priest, terrified of his maker. This poor man, abandoned by his mother in the first place because of Catholic dogma, who showed no faith at all during my life, was still haunted – and hunted – by the Catholic devil in his last moments.

He cried and begged; he didn't want to burn in hell. The way he'd lived, the pain he'd caused other people . . . He *knew*.

The priest came, absolved him. It was so strange to me. But at least my dad relaxed, comforted by the ritual, free from 'sin'.

But the pain Tony O'Sullivan caused, it wasn't his only legacy. My dad taught me lots of things: how to be suspicious, how to be distrustful, how to hate. He put me in danger, left me for the jackals like Bob, and put his addictions first, right to the end. That is all true.

But he is also the one who gave me books, who showed me how to read them and impressed on me a love of knowledge and a thirst for it that gave me a gateway out of that life. When I was a kid my dad would throw a book over, landing it on the couch beside me or on the floor, and say, 'Read that, learn about Russia.' I'd find myself engrossed in a novel about the Cold War, picking up history as I encountered tense life-and-death situations, both between the covers and, it sometimes felt, when I came back to the real world.

My dad is the one who played music and sang and pulled us up to dance in our bare feet on the carpet of our house, among the cans and piles of clothes and sadness. I do the same with my own boys now, suddenly filling the house with music and dancing with them, throwing the schoolwork to one side and reminding them that, after all, we only have a short time here so we should have fun with it.

And Tony is the one who took my son to Ireland and showed him what stability was, and peace. He is the one who gave me freedom and, frankly, the inspiration to study, by always being there to mind my son and always being so proud.

We asked my dad to hang on for my brother Michael to come and he did. But in the end it was just me and him. I sat vigil with him in a quiet ward. In the middle of the night, I watched his breaths, counting the time between them. The repetition made me drowsy. One two three four. I started to tip into sleep. But I felt it, like the energy being sucked from the room. I stared at my dad, and he breathed again. And that was the last time.

Dead?

He was dead.

It felt like my chest was being pulled open by the force of that.

Please, Dad. Please don't leave me.

But he left me anyway.

21

She looked like every woman who ever sat on the other side of the world from me. Every teacher, every lecturer, every doctor, inspector, care worker, policewoman. Women who had made my life hell, women who had judged me, held me back, pushed me down and hurt me; and like the women who had helped me, trained me, egged me on, told me to keep going. She looked like all of them.

Mary Robinson, the first female president of Ireland, represented all the women who were on the other side from people like me. The side where kids slept soundly with stomachs that were not starving for food and skin that was not starving for a kind touch, the side where the police didn't hammer on the door, where parents didn't need to be minded or scolded like mine did.

Mary Robinson looked and sounded like every woman I had ever looked up to, either in fear or with hope. She was on the other side of the world from me. Until now. Now, she was standing right in front of me looking me dead in the eye and speaking to me. My eyes filled with tears.

Dave was wearing a suit we had bought to attend a friend's wedding years before. He looked great and so did I. We had walked across town, a good-looking couple, to the gates of Trinity College where I was going to be awarded a doctorate in psychology.

'I've told you the story about them gates,' Dave said, pointing as we passed through them. He had been on the carpentry team that was called in after some madman drove through them in a rage. I let him tell it again, the familiarity of his voice soothing the rumbling nerves in my stomach that came every time I walked through here.

Dave's story, his presence, didn't fully drown out my inner demons. It was my third graduation from Trinity, but I still felt like an imposter.

Same old voice in my head, *You don't belong here.*

Many times, I'd talked to myself, told myself that I *did* belong there, I was as entitled to learn as anyone else, I'd earned my place there. I'd crawled from the bottom of the trenches to this room. I told myself all the time that nobody deserved to be here more than me. But I didn't *believe* it.

Intellectually, I knew that I had the right to take my place among the people there because I had been judged on my work and that was what was important. The papers I had written in the nine years I had been at Trinity had been marked fair and square. Those firsts – the papers that I wrote with the knowledge I'd found in books there in the vast library in Trinity College – I deserved them. I knew it but why couldn't I feel it?

Probably because I kept being reminded that I lived in a city with a hidden class system. Ireland pretends it doesn't have class, and systemically perhaps it doesn't, but the population divides itself into a cruel caste system and, depending on which side of the street you live on, you *are* judged.

Not long before I stood up to receive my doctorate, I had been admonished by a student for stepping out of line. Pulled up for being in the wrong place. Pretending to be there when we both knew people like me shouldn't be in Trinity.

'Em, sorry, but there's a class on here now,' she had said to me. A mature student in her forties, wearing the middle-class uniform of florals and a brown bob.

'Oh yeah?' I had said, putting down the stack of chairs I was lifting out of my way and looking at her. I wondered who she thought she was looking at, my hair in a messy bun, my hoodie and jeans.

Who did she see?

'You can't clean in here now,' she said, 'we have class.'

'I know,' I said, 'I'm teaching it.'

And even though she was embarrassed, apologetic,

even though she giggled and sat back in her seat with a red face, she wasn't wrong, was she? Was I really the cleaner, or was I the teacher? Studying and passing exams, did it change me? Was I so obviously working class, even now?

So yes, on the day I stood up in line with my class-mates and made my way into the hall where I was to be made a Doctor of Psychology, I still felt like I was an imposter.

My stomach filled with butterflies. *I don't belong here.* I took the steps anyway, moved forward, and suddenly I looked up and I was on the stage with Mary Robinson in her gold and red robes. She spoke to me in Latin as she handed me my doctorate.

. . . *Doctor in Philosophia . . . auctoritate mihi concessa admitto te ad gradum . . .*

There was something in her intonation, the way she looked at me, I felt like she could really see me.

Not the kid of drug addicts.

Not the gymslip mum.

Not the unfit mother.

Not the cleaner.

Me.

Mary Robinson was looking at *me*. The real one. The one even I only caught glimpses of. She was looking at the kid who battled on, the one who was hungry but ignored it, the one who read and danced and sang anyway. It was as if she could see all the stages I had come through to be here, as if my soul was visible.

And I knew she was proud of me. I could see it in her warmth, in the way she tried to stress and put meaning into the Latin words so the sense came across even if I didn't understand them. She handed me my doctorate and shook my hand and in that moment I felt that there wasn't any difference between us. I was equal. I was the same.

As I stood there shaking her hand, absorbing the ancient language, it became clear that I was enough. The only person who thought I didn't belong here, that was me. I wanted that for every woman I knew who was like me. I wanted them to know this feeling. I wanted equality for everyone.

I gave Mary Robinson a warm thank you and moved along the line to leave the stage. As I did, I caught Dave's eye. And something shifted, the walls, the crowds, the stage, it all fell away, and it was suddenly just about me and him. The way our eyes met, I could feel it, there *was* someone on this earth who really knew me, and *he* loved me. Dave, this great person, this kind and clever man, I was everything to him. I felt another surge, this time a recharge.

I felt like I'd reached the end of something, moved through the final gate, worn out and devastated, but finally whole. I had what I needed from this place. What was missing was found. I had safety, I had love, I had a family and I had my own mind. I had climbed out of the trenches I was born into. And at the end of that long and careful climb, turned out I just wanted to be with Dave and my kids.

I nearly ran off the stage, so strong was the urge to get to them. With them was where I belonged; it had taken me so long to find the door because I'd been so lost and so caught up in finding my way. I wasn't surprised to see Dave on the other side as I turned the handle. Of course, that was exactly where I was supposed to be.

It was amazing to have the choice. It was amazing to choose that instead of being pushed into it by circumstances. My happiness, it turned out, was in a small place, my little home, not in this big cold hall full of history and books. The wings that had been clipped over and over had grown back without me realizing it, and despite my addiction to flying, it turned out that I was a home bird after all.

This part, academia, this would be what I do, but they – my family – they are who I am. My parents, my brothers and sister, my husband and my kids, the people who showed me the way, the people who stopped me, hurt me, the ones who pushed me down, the ones who pulled me up, all of them made me who I am.

I knew instantly that I was no longer going to try to 'fit in', because that was impossible – I would always be a misfit to those who expect the world to only appear one way. I could do nothing about it. *From now on*, I decided, *I will be me*. I am the sum of all of my experience, and I knew I would live that truth from now on.

Katriona Marianne O'Sullivan.

Pissy pants. Smelly. Dirty child. Trash. Thick bitch. Mouth. Gymslip mum. Sponger. Waster. Common. Slut. Slapper. Stupid. Stupid. Stupid. Stupid.

PhD.

Daughter. Wife. Mother.

All these words were part of me, part of my story, and I was going to tell it. I was going to wrap my arms around that kid, that teenager, that young, lost, broken-hearted woman, and say, 'I've got you, you're all right.' Because I was.

I stepped off the stage, keeping my eyes on Dave. The old floors of Trinity's exam hall – the place that I had thought mattered – passed under me as I walked down the aisle to my family. As I took my little boy into my arms, Dave stood up and grabbed my hand, and we walked down through the hall into the beams of Dublin sunlight.

'Well, Doctor,' he said, 'what will you do now?'

'Go home with you,' I said.

22

My mother died three years after my dad. By then I was working in Trinity in a post-doctoral position, coordinating the very access programme that got me there in the first place. Tilly had been drinking a lot, perhaps not able to cope with the regrets of her life, or the loss of my dad.

I suspect that when we were small, she could always promise herself to get clean soon, stop drinking tomorrow, and told herself that we would all be okay once she did. But she never did, and we grew up and all of us had problems in our lives. I imagine the guilt was tough to bear. Tilly wasn't stupid, she knew our childhood had lasting repercussions.

Being English, there wasn't much to keep her in Ireland and so she moved back to Birmingham. To be honest, I was glad of it. With her out of the country I knew it wouldn't be me who would receive the call from the police or A&E.

If I could only ever have one memory of Tilly – instead of this conveyor belt of heartbreak and highlights – it might be this one. A year into my post-doc job as a co-ordinator of research, I was coming into my own. I was really understanding my own potential, developing programmes and speaking out. One day I was in Goldsmith Hall working away, listening to the radio on my headphones, and I was standing at the window looking out into Pearse Street when a song by Eminem called 'Headlights' – which he wrote about his own mother, who was an addict – came on. The words of the song hammered into my heart; I rang my mum.

Whenever I called my mum, she would always answer in this apprehensive way, because she knew I was listening out for signs she was drunk. She knew that I knew that she knew what was going on. That was always between us when I called her. But somehow this day I rang and there was no edge in it. As soon as she answered, I said, 'Mum, I want to ask you something.'

'Okay,' she said.

'Did you ever love me?' I said. When I asked, it was as if the words freed themselves from my throat, it felt so easy to say, though I'd wanted to ask for years.

It was like she was relieved; I could feel her relax through the phone. I'd wanted to ask for years, and she had wanted to answer.

'Oh God,' she said, 'I loved you with all my heart, I just found it really hard to show it.'

It felt honest. It felt right. I knew it wasn't a line.

'And I suppose,' she continued, 'I loved drugs more.'

It felt like a eureka moment, right then, but I know it wasn't. I know years of my therapy and learning led up to that moment, that question. The change in me felt abrupt, but it was more like the click of a closing door that has been slowly pushed shut. As a child I'd thought if I had all the information and knew what my mum and dad were up to at all times, that somehow I might save us all. I'd pushed and spied and argued with them. I'd tried so hard to save them. But at that moment, all my training and work on myself concluded with the know-ledge that I could only save myself.

I never got in the ring with my mum again after that. I let her be. I'm glad that happened before she died. That conversation was a huge part of my final healing.

In the end she had a varices bleed, the same horrific illness that affected her at thirty-nine, where your stomach bleeds and fills up and you can die. My brothers said her death scene was like something from a horror film. I was so sorry she went that way. And so sorry that after her death I found texts on her phone and discovered she had gone back on heroin in her last months. My heart went still in my chest when I realized, it was just unimagina-ble. I thought of how she had been on her last visit to us, how quiet and distant she was. I had recognized something was going on, but I wasn't able to put my finger on it. She went out one day for the longest time. But I didn't think of heroin.

I was – I am – just so sorry for her. Sixty years old, lost again to drugs. When I heard she was failing I went to see her.

'Do you need anything from me, Mum?' I said to her as she lay there, looking like a baby bird, tiny in the bed, with her huge bare eyes and her big nose.

She shook her head, and then she giggled and said, 'Oh, I think I've pushed myself this time, Kat. I have to stop or I'll die.'

I said, 'I think you've gone too far this time, Mum,' in good humour, and she looked up at me. She nodded and giggled again and said, 'I know,' and that was the last conversation we ever had. I did her hair for her, like she always loved me to, kissed her translucent paper skin, loving the smell of her, the feel of her tiny bones in my arms, and said goodbye.

I got a call a while later. Tilly was gone. I roared.

At her funeral I spoke and said, 'My dad is often credited with my success, they say I got his brains, but what my mother gave me I cherish more: she gave me the confidence to say "fuck you" when I need to, and I thank her for that.'

At first, there was a sense of relief, a calm in my life that I had never had before. I threw myself into my family and my work. Finally, I could look to the future and stop raking over my past.

But the upset came to get me eventually. Suddenly, as I chewed and swallowed a piece of apple, standing in the office at Trinity, I felt as though I was choking. I really did. I clutched my throat and called for help.

'I can't breathe,' I told my colleagues in huge, panicked sobs. My lungs filled and emptied over and over. My colleagues reassured me I wasn't choking; they could see I was breathing. Some of them recognized what I was going through. It was a huge panic attack.

I was suddenly deep in the loss of my mother; I couldn't avoid it any longer. It wasn't grief – that came later, at that point I didn't miss her – but for the first time in my life, I didn't have anyone to blame. You see, I'd had these anxious feelings all my life, and while my parents were alive, I assigned these feelings to their behaviour. And while Tilly was still alive my anxiety still made sense: she was difficult and problematic and in trouble. I was anxious because of her.

It was as though shaking my head at my mother kept my head on. As long as I had all of that wildfire blazing over there to look at, I could ignore the flames around my own feet.

When she was gone, and the anxiety was still with me, it made no sense. Finally, I could feel the red-hot heat of the fire blazing at my own feet. I got help: for the first time in my life I went on medication and the effects of it were so positive that my doctor and I realized I had been living with low-level depression, possibly for my whole life.

Something haunts me, though. I was so adamant that the way to help my mother was to insist that she stayed totally clean. I had such faith in the AA's twelve-step programme, and in abstinence being the only way to recover. But now I realize that my mother had a mental health issue that caused her highs and lows, and being completely clean made it harder for her to manage her life. That was why she fell off the wagon so quickly when things got tough. She should have been supported by doctors and medicated but we were all so sure of the opposite. I would give anything to go back, knowing other approaches to recovery I've learned about since, and get my mum on a low-level sedative that would have helped her manage her mental health. That gets me sometimes.

Epilogue

As a society we love a rags-to-riches story, and we love to see someone triumph through sheer grit and determination. But the truth is, the story is rarely that simple. My story isn't, anyway.

As part of writing this book, I wrote a list of all the people in my life. I wrote down the stories I had about each of these people, the impact they'd had on me then and how it affects me still. And as I wrote about my life in this way, I started to see something, a common thread – it was as if every now and again on my path a person stepped on to it with me and helped me along the way.

Some of the people on my list pushed me, some of them pulled me. Some of them stayed with me and some of them watched me go. I started to see my life like a series of stepping stones across a river. There were times when I didn't think I could make the next jump, or when I couldn't even see the next stone to jump on to, and always someone would appear to show me how to jump or where to go. One or two practically placed the stone down right in front of me and pushed me on to it. All of them saw past my circumstances. They saw *me*.

Teachers have a huge impact on the children they teach: it can be negative, or it can be life-changing. Mrs Arkinson gave a small frightened child a sense of dignity and sowed a seed of belief in what I could do and be. My English teacher Mr Pickering's support, the simple act of encouraging a frustrated, impoverished teenager to read and think and talk, set in motion an addiction to the rewards of learning that would see me graduating with a doctorate from Trinity fifteen years later. And in my early days at Trinity, Irena steered me towards a degree course and, at a crucial moment, she went out of her way to make sure I didn't drop out.

For most of my life I felt like I was at the bottom of a trench. The shame of poverty made it feel like I was wading through deep water alone, but the crucial thing I have learned while writing my story is that, in the tough times, I was being carried. I didn't climb out of the trench myself – I was pulled out. Of course, I worked hard, but without the network of community groups and government schemes, the funding, the Trinity Access Programme, the support offered from the college and the state, paired with friends like Joe Dowling and Audrey and my wonderful support network in Dublin 1, there isn't a chance I could have made it at all.

It is extraordinary to think of how lucky I have been.

Because I know where I would be if those people hadn't appeared when they did, if they hadn't liked me, or seen something in me that made them want to help.

I wanted to write this book to put my memories somewhere, to share them, and most of all to perhaps give hope to someone like me. I don't want to be anyone's poster child or 'success story'. I don't want to be spoken about as if I did it all by myself when I didn't. If I hadn't had all of that compassion from other people, and if they hadn't been so set on pushing this angry, hopeless girl up the banks of that trench, I wouldn't be anywhere at all.

Nothing has changed since I was a child. I see people like me still struggling to make ends meet, playing the system to survive. I know that I had some luck – I ended up in a city which was thriving, and there was funding for outreach programmes aimed at supporting the poor to do better. And I think about how quickly these started to get squeezed or shut down once the boom times were over. The divide between the rich and poor is growing; it's harder now for the poor to get an education like I did. Once again people like me must be grateful to be given stepping stones at all.

The services I was able to take advantage of, those are mostly gone now. The courses in personal growth, basic education, physical and mental development, parenting, they are all gone. The little drop-in information centre where Joe was based has become part of a wider service. The back-to-education allowance, as it was then, is gone. The Trinity Access Programme has gone from being a welcoming place for anyone who has the passion to learn, to being somewhere that seeks your credentials before even considering you for entry. A girl like me could not march over there now and knock on the director's door demanding a chance to change her life.

Poor people like me, and my parents, are still getting lost to drugs in the same percentages as forty years ago. Science has never fully been able to understand why a healthy man or woman will use a substance until they bleed to death. And there is still no understanding as to why – even when it almost kills them – the addicts return to it again and again.

People talk about addiction like it's a moral issue, that addicts like my parents are simply people making bad choices, that they're just selfish. As a kid, that's what it felt like to me too. The ambulance men who came into our house saw things that way – they saw addiction as an offence to society. And they saw me and my siblings as part of a low order and believed we didn't deserve sympathy or care either. They saw the chaos of our lives as something we brought on ourselves.

Others will tell you addiction is a disease, something

incurable, that addicts are wired that way and prone to substance abuse, and they need psycho-pharmacological intervention and understanding. They will tell you that you cannot blame an addict any more than you can blame someone with epilepsy.

My own view is that addiction is a combination of family history, trauma, biology and the weight of societal pressures and judgements. It is driven by a desire – not for the substance itself but for the escape from the pain of trauma and the consequences of poverty. My education has taught me that the parts of our brain which deal with behavioural control and with pleasure fire differently depending on the environment we are raised in. There is ample research showing that the brains of babies raised in poverty, dysfunction and trauma fire differently to those of babies brought up in loving, nourishing environments. Babies like me – babies like my parents – have brains that are more susceptible to pleasure and less able to control these drives. There are biological and social processes which make it harder for people like me to say no to drugs, sex and alcohol – even when we know it is bad for us.

There are many times in my life when I have turned away from what was 'good' for me, behaving in ways that were self-destructive – like the time I went on a bender before my exams. I know now that some of these actions were just about how my brain was wired. Chaos and stress were familiar to me, I was returning to my set point. Thankfully, along the way there have been people in positions and with funding to throw me a lifeline. Without lots of support, like I had, people coming from backgrounds like mine will continue to get addicted and live in chaos.

We live in a deeply unequal society and the groups who suffer cannot be completely blamed for the set points they maintain to survive. It would help to break the cycle if we could stop judging people and make policy to tackle the root causes of addiction. I know there will be people reading this thinking that I am justifying bad behaviour, asking: *What about personal responsibility?* My education has taught me that choice is a myth: our path is set by our history and it is very rare for someone to change that path. I am one of the lucky few who escaped the destiny set for me by my parents' addiction.

The title of this book – *Poor* – is meant to get under your skin. Depending on your background you may shudder with recognition, or think of donating to a charity, or believe it's natural that some people are at the bottom of the heap and there's no point in beating yourself up about it. 'Poor' cuts through a lot of jargon – words like 'disadvantaged', 'underprivileged', 'deprived', 'under-class'. Words that have their place but don't capture the visceral truth of what it is to grow up the way I did. The way thousands of children are growing up right now.

Being poor affects everything you do and everything you are. Thinking of poverty, we picture barefoot children in rags on the street. Of course, it is the lack of money and material possessions. For me it was those things; for so much of my life I literally had nothing. But 'poor' for me was also feeling like I had no worth. It was poverty of mind, poverty of stimulation, poverty of safety and poverty of relationships. Being poor controls how you see yourself, how you trust and speak, how you see the world and how you dream.

Even as an adult the ripples of that still affect me. I feel guilty for how we were raised. I hate to admit this – residual shame is so hard to shake – but I didn't start to brush my teeth regularly until I was in my twenties. It didn't enter my head to, unless I was handed a toothbrush like we were in Keresley Grange and directed to the sink. Even in that case I only pushed it back and forth on the front two. If you aren't shown, you don't know.

My brothers and I sometimes talk about visiting the dentist as adults and how humiliating and difficult it is to be scolded for not looking after our teeth. In the dentist's chair your background is exposed. *Your parents didn't look after you. You were not loved. You have no value.*

Being a child in poverty is the greatest indicator that

you will suffer from asthma, cancer, heart disease or mental illness, that you will go to prison, be addicted to drugs, get divorced, die young or commit suicide. Despite the understanding of all of this that we have as a society, we still allow children to go to school hungry, we still let them live in danger where drugs and alcohol are used.

Despite what we know, we still pretend that all it takes to succeed is hard work. The world keeps telling people 'Yes, you can!' when the truth is that only the privileged can. As a kid and a young adult, I felt fully responsible for being poor. And when I got out of poverty through education, the system rewarded me and heralded me as someone who had worked hard enough to do it. But the truth is, I beat the odds because I played the system and I could only do that, then, because of the amount of money available in the country.

We cannot keep pretending it's an equal opportunities education system. It is not. It's easy to go to college and build a career when there is money behind you. It's impossible to do so when there is not. For one child to be able to purchase books and equipment with no stress, and another to have nothing at all, is not a fair system. And when a child doesn't have a parent capable of funding the expense of a third-level course, which might mean additional transport and accommodation costs, that's not fair either. Many people seem to believe that

it's laziness or lack of motivation that sees kids leave
school early or drop out of college, if they even start,
but it's a question of access. And when there is no money
behind a person, the state needs to level the playing
field.

Coming from poverty, dreams aren't sky high. Most
of the time they barely go past the ceiling of a council
house. The ideas I had of 'making it' as a kid were on *Top
of the Pops* or in the cinema. And being 'better', in my
eyes, meant having a job or not selling drugs. Nobody
ever told us that we had a right to education. And the kid
I was didn't understand what an education was. I thought
it was grades, like being first in a quiz or winning at a
match. I had no idea it could make the world easier to
navigate. I didn't realize that it could change your entire
viewpoint, that an education is more than just a job. You
gain a qualification or a degree, but you also develop a
way of thinking.

I had no idea of my potential because nobody looked
at me as someone who would study. Getting me to my
GCSEs was the only goal even the teachers who cared
had for me. They considered that to be the educational
ceiling for kids like me. Poverty in a class system that we
have openly in the UK, and camouflaged here in Ireland,
weighs children down. I was weighed down by my status
for sure, as a poor kid of the underclasses in one of the
poorest cities in the UK. Most of the time being poor

felt like a sodden blanket was lying heavy across my shoulders, dragging me down into dark waters.

The Trinity Access Programme played a huge part in my journey. It changed my life, held out a hand when I was trying to climb out of the trenches. I am hugely grateful to the programme. And for many years, because I was so grateful, I championed the programme blindly. I used to give talks to potential funders, telling them my story. I'd dress the part – flowery knee-length dresses from Oasis, tights, kitten-heeled shoes, clothes I didn't like – to show how much I had *changed*. I played someone who had 'escaped' the working classes. I didn't see the problem for a while; being asked to represent the college was like a pat on the head or a gold star.

But being educated has given me the ability to think, and with it came the opportunity to critically consider society in a different way. I asked myself what was it that these access programmes offer, what do they do? And when I did that, I saw things with new eyes.

When I was studying in the programme I was a popular student, the staff liked me. I was enthusiastic and I did well, and because of that I was supported and encouraged. I was given information about grants and bursaries and helped to get them; I got a scholarship to Trinity, childcare support. I was a good-news story.

My opinion changed when I started to work as part of

the TAP team. I began to understand that a charitable mindset shaped and directed the programme. I began to see that the system that worked for me because I was 'good' was failing others who were deemed 'not good'. I realized that the students who were celebrated were the people who got good grades, who toed the line and played the part, like I had. They were grateful to be in Trinity, worked their arses off to keep up with their studies and were always keen to demonstrate that they were making the most of the opportunity. They allowed themselves to be paraded like show ponies at fund-raising events. While those students did well, the other ones, the ones who struggled more and did less well, weren't invited to these events, and at staff meetings they were spoken of in hushed tones. I figured out that only a certain type of poor person is welcome at Trinity, and that is the one who never tries to rise above the programme and remains eternally grateful for the charity it offers. Once I started to see those things, I couldn't unsee them.

Looking back, I realized that tucking the access students across the road from the main campus was telling. It might not have been intentional, it might have been a practical option that seemed to work, but I couldn't help thinking there was something deep in that decision — locating the poor students away from the main body of Trinity. It has a subconscious effect on the students themselves: unseen, unheard, unwanted.

Access programmes are a Band-Aid on a broken education system, often run by the middle classes and funded by the elite, neither of whom can fully understand what it is like to be discriminated against, either in education or in life. These programmes ask applicants to prove their poverty, prove their inequality, prove their worthiness, prove their motivation, prove their potential. And it selects the ones it believes are worthy of the 'gift' of an education.

The more I thought about it, the harder and harder my job got. I saw things that made it impossible to stay working in Trinity and in the Trinity Access Programme. I saw the project sold as one that saves poor people from the clutches of their own communities. Rich people donated, brows furrowed with concern, but their donations were not always about making lives better; it was about being identified as a Trinity donor, maybe patting themselves on the back a little and changing nothing. Indeed, wittingly or unwittingly, these structures uphold and reinforce inequality.

Many times when I stood there, appealing to Trinity alumni to dig deep for the poor, I may have been the smartest person in that room. And that's kind of the problem. I graduated with first-class honours from Trinity College *despite* growing up in a poor household. Being poor? That helped me get where I am today. And yet, even with my PhD, my new research role in Oxford

University, my prestigious Research Council funding, I knew I was still regarded with pity by the upper echelons of Trinity and by its well-heeled alumni as one of their charity cases.

What bothers me most about that way of thinking in educational institutions – because it's not unique to Trinity – is that it ignores the value of diversity. Diversity brings power.

An education is and should be for every person who wants one. And when there are barriers – finances, transport, attendance problems, caring responsibilities, complicated home lives – the challenge is to come up with solutions. Educational institutions need to consider their responsibility to help struggling students. Although the 'same' opportunities are open to people of all backgrounds, we live in a system where those coming from stable, secure childhoods do well and there is no allowance for the struggle of those who don't. We need equity in education, not equality. If someone can't see straight because the world is falling in around them, we need to raise them up to clearer skies. That is something Irena knew when she met me that first day in the TAP office.

It isn't a coincidence that people from my community are the street sweepers, cleaners and service workers, while people from the middle classes are the doctors and lawyers. That is not because of a difference in intelligence. It's because of opportunity, money and support. The middle classes are born with those three things in spades; the poor are born with none of them. And the truth is, we are losing some brilliant minds in the trenches of poverty.

I am grateful to have had those stepping stones laid out in front of me at the right time, and I am grateful to have been in the right place to take those steps and get my education. But my gratitude won't get in the way of what must be said. This poster child will tell you straight: I was lucky, the timing for me was right – I managed but so many others don't. The world is less because of that. The education system can and should do better. We *all* should do better.

Sometimes, even these days, I feel like an interloper. I need reassurance sometimes that I am okay. Deserving. Worthwhile. It's the legacy of my childhood, a legacy that the system doesn't rush to change. I try to love myself and accept it – this is who I am.

I swim every week off a beach in Howth. It's a cove my dad brought us to as kids on those few occasions when we took the ferry back to Dublin to see my grandparents.

The beach is stony and so the walk down to the water is hard and awkward, but I go barefoot and I take my time to find the gaps between the pebbles for my feet, to avoid the pain. It's not always possible to avoid it, and even if I do, the sharp freeze of the Irish Sea comes at the end anyway. I ignore the temptation to step back from it, and I wade in until the water is over my head. There is always that moment when the cold shocks me and my lungs expand and I want to get out, but I brace myself and move forward, and it passes. The sea traces a cold line around my entire body, and I know exactly where I start and where I finish. For that moment I am just Katriona – just me – and I need nothing but that. That is when I start to swim.

There is a seal there, often. He pops his head up in the way seals do, having a look, keeping tabs on the beach. I hear they bite but I am not afraid of him. I swim anyway. When we were kids on that beach with our dad he used to point at a seal and say, 'See him? That's my seal.'

We would look in amazement, totally entranced.

'You've a seal, Dad?' I'd say.

'Yep,' my dad would say. 'That's Charlie. He's my seal.'

The seal seemed to come back to see us every time we were there.

'Ah look, there's Charlie come to see us again,' my dad would say. Everything always felt good in Ireland when we were kids; my dad was calmer there, happier.

When I swim, the walk I take down the beach to the water, it brings me into myself, stops me thinking, and I need that. So much of my time I spend in this haze of what could have been, what should have been, regret, remorse and wishful thinking. But as I make my way down the sand, stepping gingerly to avoid the rocks, I know what I'm doing and what I'm moving towards. And as I approach that inevitable moment when I want to say *Not today* – as we all do when facing something tough – I know I'm going in the right direction. It's like all of those other times in my life when I was facing a hard road, when I was pregnant with my amazing son John, when I was in Trinity, when I was studying for a PhD while raising two babies and caring for my needy parents – I knew I was going in the right direction. And I kept going.

I'm always grateful for the opportunity to make my way down that stony path, to get into the cold water over my head. It reminds me who I am and where I have been. It is a reboot, a reset. I love how it feels, and the taste of the salt and the goodness of the sea lasts for hours.

And the seal is still there. The seal that belonged to my father. The exact same one that always popped up to see us when we came home. When I see him I'm transported to that moment of magic my dad gave us, that fairy tale.

My husband laughs at me, tells me that most seals don't live that long. Dave is a realist.

But I like the joke. Or maybe I want the magic. In the world I choose to live in, the seal comes to see me when

I swim because the seal belongs to my father. He is a link to him. When I see the seal I remember what I came from, who I am and what could have been.

It's a funny thing, I still get stuck in the mud sometimes, I still get weighed down by resentment and I get so angry, still, at Tony and Tilly's choices. Those feelings, like the sharp stones on the beach, get in my way if I don't negotiate them slowly.

Then that seal pops up and all the resentment and anger melts away and I miss both of them so much I can't speak. Nothing they did was right, but I love them both so fiercely despite all of it. I think that love is the purest of all. I know that I was a child of addicts, and I could only save myself. But by saving myself I saved something of them too.

In writing this book I found out more about myself than I think I wanted to, remembered more than I wanted to and got to know my parents all over again in a whole new way. And honestly? It has hurt like fuck.

But it's done. It's down. It's off my shoulders and in these pages and now it's not heavy at all. And I can share it with you and then leave it down on the shore and swim free.

On the beam.

Acknowledgements

Dave, without you, this book would not have been possible. I am forever grateful for the life we have built together and for the support you have given me in writing this book. You encourage me every day to be who I am. Thank you for the John Player Blues, for the Mitsubishi Lancer, for our children, for holding me through the dark nights and for loving me even when I couldn't love myself.

To my boys, John, Seán and Tadhg, you are my greatest achievement, and this book is your permanent record of who your mum is. Thank you for the support and for the distraction. Not forgetting my lovely daughter-in-law Sarah, thank you for bringing our little love into the world – this book is dedicated to the cycle we have broken in our family. To the successes in the next generation of O'Sullivan-Brennans.

To the many women in my life who support me – thank you! To my mother-in-law, Steph. To my sister-in-arms, Lynn Ruane – you encourage me every day to get up, to get on and to believe in myself. This book would never have happened without you. To Cliona, to Irena, to Holly, to Neasa, to Sarah-Jane Mc, to Justine H, to Audrey C, to Karen, to Ayoma, to Gemma, to Corey, to Amanda, to Mairead – to all the women who have inspired me to share my story – this book belongs to all of you.

To Liosa Mc, your support in writing this and your use of 'prose' was more than I could have ever asked for. 'Editor' does not nearly encapsulate what your role was in this book – you reminded me throughout that I am a superhero and you helped me tell this story with the compassion I feel – thank you. Patricia and Penguin – thanks for asking me to write this and encouraging me to tell the truth about what it is like to be poor.

I want to thank the people who continue to uphold the unequal structures in society – you provided me with the unending motivation needed to write this book. I hope you read this and know who you are, and that your guilt motivates you to make the world a fairer place for people like me.

Finally, I want to thank my mum and dad. I know you would be proud of the words I have written; even though you struggled, you were immensely proud of me. Thank you for the gift of music and books, for loving John like he was your own, for the fight and for the ability to say *FUCK YOU!* I will love you forever.

List of pseudonyms

The number in brackets beside each name indicates the chapter where the character is mentioned/first mentioned. Names are in alphabetical order.

Amy Gallagher (2); Anne Murphy (16); Ashley (15); August (3); Ben (10); Bett Clarke (2); Bob (3); the Clarke Family (2); Clive (7); Cynthia (10); Dan Walker (13); Danielle (14); Danny (18); Danny Roberts (10); Derek (15); the Dixon family (2); dreadlocks girl (19; fictionalized description); Eoin (14); the Gallagher family (2); Grace (6); James O'Sullivan (2); Jay (13); Jerry (10); John Bean (1); Jonno (14); Katie Gallagher (2); Kay (11); Lindsey (18); Liz (17); Luke Healy (10); Margo (15); Marian (14); Marius (17); Mark (19); Matthew O'Sullivan (3); Michael O'Sullivan (2); Mikey (15); Miss Hall (3); Mr Higgins (10); Mrs Smythe (7); Pat (14); the Patel family (2); Paul (14); Phil Parker (6); Sadhbh (19); Samuel (15); Sharon (7); Sharon Gallagher (2); Suzanne (19); Thomas (15); Tim (6); Trish (15).